Open Every Door

Mary Mottley – Mme. Marie de Tocqueville

For Mr Lehrer

and the NEWS hour team

Sheila

Mary was masterful in disappearing BUT I found her

SHEIM542@COX.NET

Open Every Door

Mary Mottley – Mme. Marie de Tocqueville

Sheila Le Sueur

French Correspondence Translated by
Claudine Martin-Yurth

Dandelion Books, LLC
www.dandelion-books.com

A Dandelion Books Publication
Dandelion Books, LLC
Mesa, Arizona

Open Every Door: Mary Mottley – Mme. Marie de Tocqueville, by Sheila Le Sueur
French Correspondence Translated by Claudine Martin-Yurth
ISBN 978-0-9967089-0-6
Hard Copy Version
Library of Congress Catalog Card Number 2015950177

Front & back covers & interior book design by Accurance, www.accurance.com

Dandelion Books, LLC
Printed in the United States of America
Dandelion Books, LLC
www.dandelion-books.com

"Ms. Sheila Le Sueur's epic work comes at an appropriate time. Socrates said when women assume the level of men they will be superior. Today's women are proving his point. But, it had been true all along."

—Richard R. Royer, M.D.

"Sheila Le Sueur's excellent research has brought to light an abundance of information about Alexis de Tocqueville's English wife, Mary Mottley. She emerges from this book a far more substantial figure than Tocqueville biographers have portrayed and establishes the basis for a fuller understanding of the great man himself."

—Frederick Brown, Author, *Alexis de Tocqueville, Letters from America*

"A wonderful glimpse into the history of the little known woman, Mary Mottley, who was behind the very famous man, Alexis de Tocqueville. The reader is quickly drawn into the narrative by her unique warm writer's voice."

—Raymond Kettel, Professor Emeritus, The University of Michigan-Dearborn

One of the definitions of "Democracy" in *Webster's New World Dictionary* is: "equality of rights, opportunity and treatment."

In theory it sounds simple; sadly, it is so difficult for many people or nations to achieve.

Dedication

To John Adalbert Lukacs

John Lukacs, born Lukács János Albert on 31 January 1924, is a Hungarian-born American historian who has written more than thirty books, including *Five Days in London, May 1940* and *A New Republic.* Now in his eighties, Lukacs came to the United States from Hungary in 1946 as a young man fleeing the emergent Communist bloc.

He was a professor of history at Chestnut Hill College from 1947 to 1994, and held the chair of that history department from 1947 to 1974. Lukacs served as a visiting professor at Johns Hopkins University, Columbia University, Princeton University, La Salle University, Regent College in British Columbia and the University of Budapest, and Hanover College.

A major theme in Lukacs's writing is his agreement with the assertion by the French historian Alexis de Tocqueville that aristocratic elites have been replaced by democratic elites, which obtain power via an appeal to the masses.[1]

---

[1] http://oll.libertyfund.org/pages/alexis-de-tocqueville-a-bibliographical-essay-by-john-lukacs, http://www.frontporchrepublic.com/2013/10/what-you-need-to-know-about-john-lukacs/

Contents

Preface

Sometimes during our journey through life we meet people who leave a lasting impression or who may even change our lives forever. Whether we meet these individuals by chance or by destiny seems irrelevant. The fact is, *they happen,* and the magic surrounding them only seems to add more intrigue to the events that follow.

Curiously, I've discovered these individuals don't have to be alive, that is, in physical body in order for such meetings to take place. Further validation of their occurrence is revealed through strange encounters thereafter. It is like being given a treasure map and bidden to follow each clue. Why? For what reason? That is part of the mystery. You don't really know.

Yet you feel compelled, almost obsessed to stay connected to these individuals. Ultimately you may find that you invite yourself into their lives as listener and loyal friend—or even biographer, as in my case. This has been the strange and wonderful experience of my encounter with Mary Mottley, or Mme. Marie de Tocqueville.

I am originally from the Island of Jersey, one of the Channel Islands located between England and France. On June 30, 1940 when I was 13 years old, the Nazis invaded Jersey, Thus began five years of German Occupation until May 9, 1945.

During that time we lived in a state of constant fear. Nazis troops were everywhere, guarding our every move. It was a nightmare from which we all recovered, but not without permanent scars.

When World War II was finally over—when we could once again hoist the flag of Great Britain over our beloved Jersey—each of us knew without a doubt that nothing, absolutely nothing, was more important than freedom, healthy associations and active citizenry. These are the three criteria required in a democracy as described by 19th century French political thinker and historian Alexis de Tocqueville in *Democracy in America*, published in 1836 after his visit to America.

After training to be a Registered Nurse at London Hospital and working as a nurse first in the UK and then in Jersey, I answered an ad for a nursing position in Detroit, Michigan, where my aunt and uncle had been living for several years. On November 26, 1952, I arrived in the US with a green card. My mother and sister followed shortly after, and the three of us decided to stay.

On March 18, 1958, I officially became a US citizen. From 1955-1977, I was employed as a registered nurse at Bon Secours Hospital in Gross Pointe, Michigan. I then moved to Mesa, Arizona, where I continued my nursing career until retirement in 1992. By that time I had lived in the US for over 50 years.

Before retiring, I gave much thought to my future. Most people my age view this time as the sunset of their lives. I saw only the sunrise. There were no Club Med cruises in my plans! I set forth three goals for myself. I wanted to:

1. Be a more informed voter, to be confident that I would be voting for the person who resonated with my beliefs.
2. Develop an appreciation and understanding of classical music.
3. Become a better reader.

In order to achieve my first goal, I joined the New Frontiers for Learning in Retirement at Mesa Community College. With a desire to learn more about American democracy, I enrolled in a class on the Federalist papers. What I learned in that class instead was that I needed to learn a lot more about American history.

I then enrolled in History 101 with the regular students and it was a most rewarding experience. At last I had chosen the right course. I came to America at the beginning, with Christopher Columbus!

We are given many opportunities in life to become active citizens. I believe that one of the most important responsibilities as a citizen is that of exercising our right to vote. Suffrage is an important reason why democracy holds such great value for me.

In addition to learning more about the fledgling 13 Colonies' struggle for independence, the History 101 course proved to be exactly the kind of preparation I needed for watching an 11-month *C-SPAN* series on American Democracy featuring Alexis de Toqueville's book, *Democracy in America.*[2] The first program in the series had already been scheduled.

---

[2] http://www.c-span.org/series/?Tocqueville, Alexis-Charles-Henri Clérel de Tocqueville (29 July 1805, Paris – 16 April 1859, Cannes) was a French political thinker and historian best known for his *Democracy in America* (appearing in two volumes: 1835 and 1840) and *The Old Regime and the Revolution* (1856). In both of these works, he explored the effects of the

With much excitement, I knew this series was tailor-made for me. I was eager to learn how democracy actually worked here in America. What were the issues this young country had confronted at the outset? How did American Democracy, i.e., a Democratic Republic, differ from other forms of government that called itself a democracy? I hoped the *C-SPAN* series would answer these questions for me.

The text for the program was *Tocqueville in America*, by George Wilson Pierson.[3] A series of excellent videos portrayed each of the places where Tocqueville stopped to interview people and observe their lifestyles during his 1831 visit to America. Several historians and dignitaries contributed to the development of each segment of the program and local citizens participated by telling stories about their history of that area. The program

---

rising equality of social conditions on the individual and the state in western societies. *Democracy in America* (1835), his major work, published after his travels in the United States, is today considered an early work of sociology and political science.

3 http://www.amazon.com/Tocqueville-America-George-Wilson-Pierson/dp/0801855063/ref=la_B001HPC5HI_1_1?s=books&ie=UTF8&qid=1440118736&sr=1-1

also provided an excellent guided tour of parts of America I had never seen.

I found the first program fascinating. However, only after viewing the second segment that was filmed at the Château de Tocqueville in Normandy, France, did I really get excited. As the camera panned over the village of Tocqueville, past the church and over the pond where swans majestically floated by, I stared as if transfixed. Then as the Château came into view, suddenly I was overcome by a deep longing and bittersweet pangs of nostalgia. I had the impression the Château was welcoming me with open arms.

The feeling of belonging to this time and place was further confirmed for me when the camera turned toward the horizon, swept up and down the coastline and then outward to the ocean. I could feel my heart beating faster. I could almost smell the salty ocean air and in my mind's eye I could see the waves leaping up and falling back... I could see the tall spumes of water rolling over the beach, their bubbly foam darkening the sand for miles along the pristine shoreline.

For a wistful moment I was back in Jersey, reliving my early childhood—but that wasn't all. I also knew without a doubt that *Alexis de Tocqueville was very much a part of that life.* The connection I was feeling seemed even less strange and more personal when I learned that we had grown up just a short distance apart from each other. Alexis lived in Normandy and I grew up on a small Channel island off the coast of Normandy, closer to France than to Great Britain. The fact that I was born 122 years after him in 1927—he was born in 1805—didn't seem to matter in the least.

Then the actual connections started surfacing. I learned that the name of the Tocqueville family priest and tutor who raised Alexis according to Catholic and aristocratic tradition was

Abbé Le Sueur—and Le Sueur is my family name! My great-grandmother, Sophie Le Brun, was born in 1831, the year Alexis and his friend, Gustave de Beaumont sailed from the port of Le Havre to America.

Something clicked inside. Yes, I confirmed to myself. Alexis de Tocqueville was definitely a part of my life. The centuries that separated us melted away.

After viewing the entire *C-SPAN* series about Alexis de Tocqueville and American Democracy, my appetite was whetted. What was it about Tocqueville's life and his passion to understand democracy that had so captivated me? Why was it so important for me to learn more about him and about his life? It was as if I'd heard him say to me, "Follow the road ahead, open every door and you will find your answer."

Obediently I did as I was told and was ever so grateful that I had. Eight years later, in September of 2006, I found myself sitting in the kitchen of the Château de Tocqueville as the current Countess de Tocqueville, whose husband is a descendent of Alexis de Tocqueville's brother Edouard, served me afternoon tea.

Introduction

As a nurse I must have taken hundreds, maybe thousands of nursing histories, so in pursuing my research about Alexis de Tocqueville, my natural inclination was to inquire about his family. This information was easy to find. His parents, brothers and friends were well documented.

But where, I wondered, was his wife? And what about her family?

By this time, as part of enjoying the *C-SPAN* series, I had already read Pierson's 880-page book about Tocqueville in America. On page 692 I'd learned that in 1835 Alexis had married an English woman named Mary Mottley of no fortune and no particular family. That was it. End of story.

I was stunned. How could Alexis's wife have been dismissed in one sentence, just like that?

Who really was Mary Mottley?

In my determination to know more about democracy in America and Alexis de Tocqueville, even though one door after another had already opened for me, for some uncanny reason that one had remained closed. Finding the key to that particular door became my passion, or I might even say my obsession.

Although French Professor Jean-Louis Benoît, one of Tocqueville's chief biographers and archivists,[4] also mentions Mary Mottley in his books, I felt that even Dr. Benoît gave Tocqueville's wife only peremptory treatment. Why was that, I wondered. Why was I having such difficult time collecting more information about her?

---

4 Jean-Louis Benoît is a philosopher who devoted his life work to researching and writing books about Alexis de Tocqueville. In his works about de Tocqueville, Dr. Benoît refers to Mary Mottley as Mme. de Tocqueville. In chapter 9 of this book are excerpts from translated letters of Alexis to Mary which appear in *Alexis de Tocqueville - Oeuvres complètes, tome 14 : Correspondance familiale* [*Volume XIV, Family Correspondence,* Gallimard (24 mars 1998)], and are reproduced here, courtesy of Éditions Gallimard. http://www.amazon.fr/Alexis-Tocqueville-compl%C3%A8tes-Correspondance-familiale/dp/2070750655/ref=sr_1_16?ie=UTF8&qid=1439991737&sr=8-16&keywords=jean-louis+benoit

After contacting Dr. Benoît, a warm and generous person who soon became a good friend, I learned that Alexis's marriage to a commoner was one of the "scandals of the time." By avoiding the subject as adroitly as possible, most biographers and Tocqueville analysts delivered the polite message that information about Mary was not a welcome contribution to the Tocqueville family legacy. Therefore, the less said about her, the better.

I was incensed. This seemed to be highly unfair. For some reason I didn't believe Alexis's choice of a lifetime partner was wrong for him. I felt Mary Mottley must have been an admirable person in her own right, and I set about to learn more about her.

As soon as I made my decision to delve into this matter, I felt a powerful surge of energy—a sense of extraordinary excitement nothing short of a destiny call. I had given myself an assignment that I knew I was obliged to complete.

In that split second, I realized that the bond I felt with Alexis was not only through his life work about democracy; it was also through his wife, Madame Marie de Tocqueville/Mary Mottley. The mere mention of the name "Mary Mottley" sparked an immediate and inexplicable connection. Somehow my life and hers were integrally entwined and *that was the initial attraction I'd felt with Alexis through the* C-SPAN *programs.*

Alexis was inviting me to deliver his beloved Mary's story to the world.

I set to work. It took seven years of persistence with many wrong turns, but doggedly I traveled onward, browsing through books, archives, Internet websites, correspondence with countless people, until eventually all the pieces started to come together. I can honestly say that I know Mary Mottley's family and their history better than my own.

I have not been on this journey alone. Countless others, what I like to call a "cast of thousands," have traveled this road with me. My address book is filled with names of new friends all over the world. The following story describes my mission, under Alexis de Tocqueville's directive, to bring his much maligned wife back into the limelight standing next to him.

In chapter one, I provide an overview of Mary Mottley's life. In chapter two, I tell the saga of my search to gather information about Mary and why this became such a fascinating treasure hunt. In chapter three I trace the Mottley family lineage and provide considerable information about this fascinating family from Portsmouth, England.

Alexis de Tocqueville is introduced in chapter four, with sufficient background about late 18th century and early 19th century France, the Revolution, Reign of Terror and Napoleonic Era immediately preceding Alexis's birth. I also describe some of the key players in Alexis's life: his tutor, Abbé Le Sueur, Alexis's brothers and some of his good friends.

In chapter five, Mary and Alexis meet, marry and eventually settle into a blissful life together at the Château de Tocqueville. I devote chapter six to a description of the Château, where the married couple truly "lived happily ever after."

Chapter seven provides a more detailed description of Mary, Alexis and democracy in America as Alexis pursues his passion to discover how he can adapt democratic principles to a decaying yet stubbornly resistant upper class France besieged by the restless bourgeoisie and a rebellious working class.

In the 19th century, the French, like the rest of the Western world, were about to participate in an Industrial Revolution that would profoundly affect every area of their lives. In chapter eight I describe pre-Industrial Europe and America, before the automobile, train, plane, telephone and electricity had been invented. Would the life of Mary and Alexis have been radically different had they lived 100 years later—or in the 21st century? Unquestionably, yes. Both were late 19th century misfits. There was no place in the world yet for enlightened intellectuals, especially not for female ones.

As a man with a pedigree and part of the landed gentry, Alexis was free to do as he pleased. Mary, on the other hand, was a prisoner of her time. Her books, Alexis and his colleagues were her only cultural and intellectual outlets. Under the circumstances, one could say she led a richly satisfying life, yet in truth it was only vicariously through the intellectual stimulation provided by Alexis and his colleagues that she was able to experience any form of fulfillment. Development of her own potential simply was not possible.

Chapter nine is devoted to samples of Alexis's letters to Mary expertly translated from French to English by Claudine Martin-Yurth and included in this book with the permission of Éditions Gallimard.[5] Alexis's eloquent expression of devotion to his beloved wife is clearly evidenced in this correspondence and puts to rest any questions regarding the depth and breadth of their extraordinary relationship. If Mary had not burned all of her letters to her husband after Alexis's death, some of these also would have been included in this chapter. No doubt she was wise to dispose of the letters; as soon as Alexis was buried, the Tocqueville family evicted Mary from the Château and apparently tried to pretend she had never existed. One could only imagine what may have happened to her personal memorabilia that referenced Alexis had she not burned it.

[5] Op. Cit., Translated letters of Alexis to Mary which appear in *Alexis de Tocqueville - Oeuvres complètes, tome 14 : Correspondance familiale* [*Volume XIV, Family Correspondence,* Gallimard (24 mars 1998)], and are reproduced here, courtesy of Éditions Gallimard.

In chapter ten, I offer a few personal thoughts regarding Alexis and Mary, ending the book with one of several letters that I have written to Mary.

And now it is time to pull the golden cord, open the curtains and bring to center stage the hero of my story, Mary Mottley/Mme. Marie de Tocqueville.

1

Who Was Mary Mottley?

If all the world really is a stage as Shakespeare proclaimed, and each century another act delivered through scripts authored by historians and biographers, at best Mary Mottley, wife of famous 19th Century French political thinker and social commentator Alexis de Tocqueville, would have been merely a bit player.

Although it proved to be extremely difficult to obtain information about Mary beyond a few sketchy details, clearly she was the star of her husband's life. Without Mary Mottley at his side for 24 years, it is possible that Alexis de Tocqueville may have disappeared into the archives as just another outspoken voice among the many during a time when France was seething with political upheaval.

Alexis loved his wife dearly and was devoted to her, which is evidenced by the fact that he made a radical decision to go against the social mores of his family and French aristocracy by declaring to them that he planned to marry her. Mary Mottley was not even French, she had no pedigree and she certainly wasn't a wealthy member of the upper class bourgeoisie.

The French elite must have enjoyed gossiping about the couple whenever they chanced upon a juicy morsel that afforded sufficient distraction to lift them momentarily out of their boredom.

Usually when mentioned by historians and biographers, Mary was described as a sickly woman, ill tempered, and a "foreigner":

poor, plain, and Protestant. Writes Hugh Brogan in *Alexis de Tocqueville: A Life:* "She [Mary] was pretty, or Tocqueville probably never would have noticed her.... Tocqueville needed women for more than sex... he wanted mothering... he needed companionship... he needed someone who needed him: someone he could cherish and protect. In Mary Mottley he found it all. She was not perfect... she was something of a hypochondriac, perhaps because of her background in quack medicine. She had little humour and no wit, although she enjoyed a good conversation."[6]

Dr. Brogan's description of Mary was hardly flattering, but at least he gave her more than the usual peremptory one-liner that was customary for Tocqueville scholars. This is probably because I sent Dr. Brogan a large portion of the material about Mary Mottley long before 2006, the date when his biography

[6] Brogan, Hugh, Aexis de Tocqueville: A Life. Yale University Press, 2006, pp. 97,98. http://www.amazon.com/Alexis-Tocqueville-Life-Hugh-Brogan/dp/0300108036/ref=sr_1_1?ie=UTF8&qid=1439993433&sr=8-1&keywords=hugh+brogan+-+alexis+de+tocqueville

of Tocqueville was first published. In the book Dr. Brogan acknowledged me as the source for his information about Mary's family. I was pleased about this, not for the recognition but for the fact that it had been announced to the world that finally someone was engaged in serious research about Mary.

Fervently I believed Mary Mottley needed to be rescued from oblivion, and if no one else wanted to do it, I took it upon myself to complete this task before it was time for my own body to be lowered into the ground and marked with a headstone.

Although my introduction to Mary was inarguably through my fascination with Tocqueville's writings on democracy, I was determined to learn more about this "sickly plain woman" so I could make my own judgement call. How and why this obsession took hold of me, I cannot explain. All I know is that it was a directive I knew I couldn't ignore.

Some have suggested a past life connection, that possibly in another lifetime I may have actually been Mary Mottley. This idea is so foreign to me with my Catholic upbringing, I readily dismissed it. I don't believe in past lives. And yet... has Mary not appeared to me in my dreams? Did I not spend days on end digging through books and papers, contacting librarians, historians and biographers in the UK, France and the US, to learn as much as I could about this woman? Did I not make several pilgrimages to the UK and France to visit every place where Mary and members of her family lived or spent time?

And finally, at age 88, did I not pronounce to my publisher and editor, Carol Adler, that before I leave, I want to be known as the person who introduced Mary Mottley to the world by writing a book about her? "I want to set the records straight," I told Carol. "I want the world to know that Mary Mottley was a brilliant, accomplished woman who was the perfect soulmate for her famous husband."

One thing is certain. Most people retire into old age playing shuffleboard and bridge or watching TV reruns. Their only excitement may be going to the grocery store, awaiting the next visit to the doctor's, or receiving news about the passing of yet another friend.

Not me. This never would have been my life in retirement. I have always had an insatiable thirst to learn, and I know I share this quality with Mary. Researching and writing about Madame de Tocqueville and the important role she played in her husband's life has inspired me to stretch myself beyond the boundaries of ordinary life. Through my determination to learn more about this remarkable woman, I started to dwell in a part of the mind where the exigencies of this human journey became part of a large wall-size painting or fresco in which all of us are portrayed as a single global family that share the same desires. Those desires are an innate longing to be free to express our beliefs without fear of being banished or expelled from our society, and to have an opportunity as equal citizens of our respective countries to make a positive impact upon its people.

We are living in insane times. I wonder what Alexis and Mary would say if they had been alive to witness some of the events of this century: terrorist attacks, bombings, race riots, bank corruption, "bubbles" and housing foreclosures, immigration issues, drug and slave tracking, and the many other disruptive events.

Possibly they were convinced that the time they lived in was also "insane." I've often thought about this as I've compared the two eras both here and abroad. Please Mary, I invite you to join this discussion.

2

Searching for Mary

After surfing the Internet to find information about Alexis de Tocqueville's life, as reported previously, I found to my dismay that most historians dismissed Mary in one or two unflattering sentences. Others skipped over her completely.

In a sense I can understand that a historian's primary focus is on their subject matter. Why would they be interested in knowing more about the people in Alexis's personal life? Even so, for biographers of the great man to treat his wife with such deference seemed strange, almost peculiar.

I knew that 19th century women were considered inferior to their male counterparts. English naturalist and geologist Charles Darwin's conclusions were based on those of anthropologists contemporary to his time who stated they were "creatures with smaller brains than men, thus incapable of being educated."[7] Aristocratic women in France were drawing room decorations. Flanked by a staff of servants, they spent their time socializing, dressing and undressing (it took two hours for the maid to

[7] Darwin concluded that adult females of most species resembled the young of both sexes and from this and the other evidence, "reasoned that males are more evolutionarily advanced than females" (Kevles, 1986:8). Many anthropologists contemporary to Darwin concluded that "women's brains were analogous to those of animals," which had "overdeveloped" sense organs "to the detriment of the brain" (Fee, 1979:418). Carl Vogt, a University of Geneva natural history professor who accepted many of "the conclusions of England's great modern naturalist, Charles Darwin," argued that "the child, the female, and the senile white" all had the intellect and nature of the "grown up Negro" (1863:192). Many of Darwin's followers accepted this reasoning, including George Romanes, who concluded that evolution caused females to become, as Kevles postulated: . . . increasingly less cerebral and more emotional. Romanes . . . shared Darwin's view that females were less highly evolved than males—ideas which he articulated in several books and many articles that influenced a generation of biologists. Romanes apparently saw himself as the guardian of evolution, vested with a responsibility to keep it on the right path. . . . University of Pennsylvania . . . paleontologist Edward Drinker Cope wrote that male animals play a "more active part in the struggle for existence," and that all females, as mothers, have had to sacrifice growth for emotional strength . . . (Kevles, 1986:8,9).
http://www.icr.org/article/378%2525252520

lace up her corset) for salon and ballroom appearances; and entertaining their husbands in their lavishly furnished boudoirs.

Middle class women earned their living as governesses and caregivers. Lower class women were one notch higher than slaves, feeding a large family on a limited income derived from cooking, cleaning and tending to their master's domicile or their mistress's corset lacing.

Women of all classes were considered chattel or property to be exploited by their parents or husbands. The most important function of a titled maiden was to produce pedigreed heirs.

As far as Tocqueville historians were concerned, Mary Mottley was a Protestant English woman, plain looking, with an ordinary background, which meant classless and without money. She was also older than Alexis, which was frowned upon for breeding purposes. So here is the complete list: poor, plain, Protestant,

English, and older. Some even claimed she was a difficult woman—caustic and prone to be outspoken.

Repeatedly I asked myself: *would Alexis have married a woman from a lower class unless he loved her?* According to several reliable sources that my research produced, which was ultimately validated by Alexis's correspondence to his wife (see chapter 9 for translated excerpts) it was a choice that he never regretted. The marriage was good. The two had a strong bond, sharing their mutual love for learning and their eagerness to participate in the intellectual movement of Enlightenment that was sweeping across Europe and had already taken hold in America.

What I believe the male historians overlooked was the fact that a "caustic outspoken temperament" could hardly be attributed to a person who was plain and ordinary. On the contrary, temper is a sign of temperament. Such a person would also be opinionated, and if they happened to be educated, their opinions might have considerable value.

Eventually I learned that Mary/Marie came from a prominent bourgeoisie family in the southwestern part of England. She was intelligent, well-educated and fluent in several languages. No doubt she and Alexis spent countless hours having stimulating conversations. The more I learned about Mary Mottley, the more I came to realize that she was probably her husband's greatest inspiration.

Nevertheless, Mary Mottley was far from a suitable match for an aristocratic Frenchman with a prestigious pedigree.

Mary's Roots

A footnote in a book from Notre Dame University on an intra-library loan referring to family correspondence by Tocqueville listed Mary as having been born in Devon, England. It was a false lead. I later learned that Mary was born in the village of Alverstoke in Hampshire.

John Sinel, who lives in Hampshire, gave me the names and published phone numbers of families whose names were "Mottley" and "Belam." Mrs. Belam's maiden name, I'd learned, was Elizabeth Mottley; she was Mary's aunt.

The directory listings bore no fruit, but slowly I started to expand my knowledge base through the many people whom I contacted by phone. I called Alan King, the Portsmouth, UK librarian, who was extremely helpful. Diana Gregg and Ann-Marie Graham at the Portsmouth Records Office also worked diligently to provide me with answers to my questions.

Michael Rowe, librarian at the Royal Hospital Haslar where Mary's father, George Mottley, was an administrator was extremely helpful. Originally when the Haslar Hospital opened in 1753 it was a naval hospital, so I contacted the Institute of Naval Medicine, where Jane Wickenden, the Historic Collections librarian, joined my research team. Other archivists in Portsmouth helped me as well.

From the moment I mentioned my project to Bruce Barnes, librarian at the Mesa Public Library, he became an enthusiastic supporter.

Finally I received my first breakthrough from Angela Underwood, the librarian at the Société Jersiaise, in Jersey, my island home. She suggested I contact the Archives at St. Lô in Normandy. I did so, and Monsieur Leroy Janjac provided me with copies of Mary and Alexis's wedding certificate and Mary's death certificate.

The pieces to the puzzle were finally coming together! Now I immersed myself in learning about the life and times of 19th century England and France.

As I continued to learn more about Mary, I sensed that a woman of her intelligence must have had an extremely challenging time, especially since she would have been ostracized by Alexis's family as well as the intelligentsia, a closed fraternity or "Old Boys' Club."

I asked myself how I would have dealt with such rejection had I found myself in Mary's position. I also speculated about my fate as a peasant or a member of the bourgeois. Based on my station in life, how would I have responded to each of the revolts that had swept through France during the late 1700s?

I feel certain I would have been involved in the struggle for freedom and equality, regardless of my standing. And, like Mary, I would have been cheering on every courageous woman who dared to voice her opinions.

I continued to find it intriguing to look at Mary's life as a reflection of my own. How would I cope with riding in a horse-drawn carriage? If I were ill, what would the standard of care have been? What about transportation and communication? What was life like without telephones? Would I have had the opportunity for an education? How would I dress? What were the fashions during that time? The more I learned about Alexis and Mary (Marie) and their lifestyle, the more eagerly I welcomed new information. I loved the feeling of magic that continued to be the driving force that fueled my curiosity.

Time to Visit Mary

I knew I needed to visit the UK and France, to plan pilgrimages to the places where Mary was born, grew up and died, and where she and Alexis lived. Every existing location pertaining to the history of Mary Mottley was on my agenda. Between 2000 and 2009 I made four trips, during which I met many of the major academicians in the UK and France who had written books about Alexis. I also met Tocqueville descendants as well as a Sorbonne University professor who participated in the original *C-SPAN* program that featured the Tocqueville story.

Retracing Mary's Steps

Each of my "Mary Mottley Pilgrimages" to the UK and France was memorable. In the UK I had the pleasure of visiting the Royal Hospital Haslar in Alverstoke, Hampshire, England, where Mary was born and her father, George Mottley, was an agent; and also St. Mary's Church, where she was baptized. In Portsmouth, I visited the Highland Cemetery, location of the family plot.

It was a cold and dreary day. The sky was gray and overcast. Large birds circled overhead. Were they curious to see a visitor entering this forlorn and nearly forgotten place? Many of the tombstones lay crumbled and strewn on the ground. Other graves were breaking open.

Across the street I noticed a pub with the sinister name of "Grave Diggers." Stepping gingerly through the overgrown ruins, I searched for the name "Mottley" on any of the remaining stones. Finally I found the family plot.

Although the headstone had long since disappeared, I knew I was standing on the spot where Mary's brother and sister had been buried. *How strange,* I thought. *Here I am—and here they are!* The unreality of it all was difficult to grasp. I longed to ask them questions about this woman who had been the constant companion of my thoughts for so many years already. I hoped she would have been pleased to know that I am now telling her story.

At a certain point when I had gathered enough information, I realized it was time for me to fulfill my promise to Alexis. The book about Mary must be written. I presented myself with three main questions: Who was Mary/Marie, really? How could I bring her to life today, and what value would this book have for historians as well as modern lay readers?

Value was the operative word. Marie was of immense value to Alexis. I sensed he knew from the first time he met her that Mary possessed all the qualities he desired in his choice of a wife. He loved and respected her until the day he died.

This was exactly the value I sought in order to justify writing the book. Mary's intelligence, courage and strength of character made it possible for Alexis to leave the world an important legacy.

It is my honor and privilege to introduce Madame Marie de Tocqueville to the world.

3

The Mottley Family

Even in the 21st century it is not uncommon for the spouse of a famous person to be ignored by biographers and academicians unless that person is pedigreed by birth or has collected their own accolades. In the 19th century, before women's suffrage and the women's liberation movement, such dismissiveness, especially of untitled females, was the norm.

Mary Mottley was no exception. Not only was Mme. de Tocqueville a member of the bourgeoisie and consequently ostracized by her husband's aristocratic family and peers, but she was also perceived by Tocqueville's [male] biographers as a rather ordinary and not particularly accomplished individual.

For both of these reasons, Mme. de Tocqueville seems to have almost vanished from the copious annals depicting Tocqueville's professional and personal life. One finds only a few backhand remarks as if merely to acknowledge the fact that the great man had a wife.

George Wilson Pierson[8] describes Mary Mottley as an English woman of no fortune who was older than her husband, taller than him and—heaven forbid—a Protestant![9] ! In his essay, *Come Disait Monsieur de Tocqueville,* Antoine Redier[10] mentioned only that Mme. de Tocqueville had large yellow teeth. French biographer, André Jardin[11] cited her as a woman without a

[8] George Wilson Pierson (22 October 1904 -12 October 1993) was the first official historian of Yale University. He is the author of *Tocqueville and Beaumont in America* (1938) - http://en.wikipedia.org/wiki/George_Wilson_Pierson.

[9] Mary Mottley did convert to Catholicism before her marriage to de Tocqueville.

[10] A biographical study of Tocqueville, *Comme Disait M. de Tocqueville,* by Antoine Redier [Paris: Perrin, 1925].

[11] André Jardin (1912 – 1996) was a French biographer and historian, best known for his studies of Alexis de Tocqueville and 19th century French history. His 1984 biography of Tocqueville, *Alexis de Tocqueville: 1805-1859*—translated into English as *Tocqueville: A Biography* in 1988, by Lydia Davis and Robert Hemenway—was acclaimed as the definitive account of the life and career of the author of *Democracy in America.*

fortune and one with whom Tocqueville had been having an affair for several years. Skillful writers cleverly craft their innuendos. A "commoner," even if married to an aristocrat, could never be considered more than that sire's prostitute or mistress.

Often the fate of being a woman was a curse in itself. If she happened to be titled, she was still treated like chattel and matched with her perspective husband through a formal business transaction with someone of equal pedigree and/or wealth. The religious match was taken for granted, since Church and State (Roman Catholic and the Crown) were joined at the hip.

In bourgeois families, the eldest daughter was the first to be purchased by the highest and most suitable bidder. Pickings might be lean and a bit dicey for the rest of the siblings, since each needed to be packaged with a suitable dowry. Spinsters became companions, governesses or maids.

The Mottleys[12]

The Mottleys can be traced back to the 1700s through records of the early history of the county of Hampshire. Apparently the family settled in the village of Alverstoke, located in Gosport on Portsea Island, across the harbor from Portsmouth. Gosport dates back to 1180 when a merchant named Jean De Gisors, who owned land in Portsea, needed a sheltered port for his fleet of ships.

Although at the time Gosport was merely a small fishing village with few inhabitants, Jean de Gisor envisioned a big future for Gosport. It was a prime piece of real estate destined to expand and flourish throughout the maritime history of England.

By the 19th century, the city of Portsmouth had evolved into an important commercial port. It was also the location of a major

[12] The following material about the Mottley family was obtained through the professional archival services of Anthony Adolph, Genealogist, www.anthonyadolph.co.uk, and can be verified via hard copy, dated November 12, 2001, as filed in the archives of Sheila Le Sueur.

base for the Royal Navy. Residents at that time must have felt an air of expectancy and excitement as new industries and opportunities for gainful employment continued to attract a large migration from other parts of England.

It was as if the incoming tide of commercialism had engulfed the surrounding villages and hamlets. Springing up around the city was the suburban sprawl of dwellings for the middle and working classes.

In the city itself, living conditions were abominable. With swarms of workers and their families living in tightly congested unsanitary quarters, it didn't take long for the entire area to become a fertile breeding place for several of the most deadly infectious diseases. As late as 1848 an outbreak of cholera killed 638 people. At this time, asepsis and other simple preventive measures such as hand washing were unknown.

James C. Mottley, Sr. (1737-1805), Mary Mottley's Paternal Grandfather

James C. Mottley, Sr. was a bookseller and printer whose business was located in the High Street in Portsmouth.[13] Although the press mainly printed pamphlets and sermons, in 1802 they also published *The History of Portsmouth: containing its origin, progressive improvements & present state of its public buildings.* Announcement of the book was published in the *Portsmouth Telegraph*, founded by James C. Mottley, Jr., in 1799.

A daily newspaper, the *Portsmouth Telegraph* was the first of its kind. Each issue was seven pages long and cost 7 shillings per issue. The emergence of a daily newspaper indicated the spread of literacy among the middle class. It also indicated the growth of a bourgeoisie with sufficient purchasing power for such luxuries.

---

[13] *Hampshire Directory 1784 p 104, Hampshire Director 1792 p. 201; Universal British Directory* Volume IV, page 201.

A copy of the first edition of the *Portsmouth Telegraph* is on permanent display at the Portsmouth Public Library.[14] In later years the newspaper's name changed to the *Hampshire Telegraph,* and after a run of 177 years, the last issue was published in 1976.

Portsmouth Telegraph Articles

Among the archives in Portsmouth, I found several interesting articles that aptly describe 19th century English life. The following are a few samples:

==

LADIES ACADEMY

FRATTON, Jan. 10, 1801

MRS. EWINGTON takes this method of returning thanks to the Inhabitants of Fratton, for the liberal

---

[14] https://www.portsmouth.gov.uk/ext/events-parks-and-whats-on/libraries/library-information.aspx

encouragement they have given her ACADEMY, and begs leave to inform her Friends, and the Inhabitants of Portsmouth and its Vicinity, that she has taken a House in a very eligible situation at Fratton, for the purpose of accommodating TWENTY YOUNG LADIES as Borders. The strictest attention will be paid by Mrs. EWINGTON to every branch of their Education; to form the minds and morals of those entrusted to her care, and make them real ornaments of the Female Character: she not only superintends them herself during their studies, but in those hours allotted to their recreations.

⤇ The School opens again, after the present Vacation, on Monday, the 12th Instant.

N.B. The most approved Masters attend the School.[15]

=====================================

[15] Copyright, 2001, Archives Britain.

==

IMPORTANT INFORMATION

ROBBERD's BALSAMIC ELIXIR, or COUGH DROPS, for Coughs, Asthmas, and Consumptions. These Drops are justly allowed the very best Medicine in the whole World, for the certain relief and effectual cure of the above complaints.

Not an instance having occurred, (though taken by more than 30,000 Patients,) wherein they have been known to fail, so superior are their virtues over every other Medicine, that let the Patient be ever so emaciated or reduced, after having tried every Medical Assistance, together with all the Advertised Nostrums, to no purpose, it will act as it were a Charm, and instantly relieve the most inveterate Cough, give ease and freedom to Respiration, promote gentle Expectoration, strengthen the whole Debilitated Constitution,

procure the refreshing comfort of rest and sleep, and quickly effect a permanent Cure.

Too much cannot be said in praise of so valuable a Remedy, as it only requires to be known to meet with universal preference.

Sold by the Inventor and Proprietor, J. Robberds, Surgeon, Apothecary, and Man-Midwife, No. 379, Strand, London; in Bottles at 2s. and 5s 5d. each; likewise by his special appointment, by Mr. Dimmock, Winchester; Mr. Hollis, Romsey; M.C. Mottley, Portsmouth; and by the Agents to this Paper; also by one or more respectable Venders of Midicine [sic] in every town of the kingdom, where a bill may be had gratis, containing further accounts of its virtues, together with cases and references of persons of the first respectability.[16]

=====================================

---

[16] Ibid.

======================================

SALE OF A WIFE. —Lawrence Stephenson, of West Lutton, in the East Riding of York, sold his wife Jane to William Servant, of Hovingham, for five shillings (who returned two shillings and six-pence to the purchaser) in open market at New Malton, on Saturday fe'nnight, and delivered her in a halter on Monday, at the Market Cross there.[17]

======================================

[17] Ibid.

==

ROYAL HOSPITAL, AT HASLAR

THE 26TH DECEMBER, 1800.

ON TUESDAY, the 6th of Jan. 1801, at Ten

O'Clock in the Morning, will be

SOLD BY AUCTION,

By JOHN STEAD,

Several Lots of

BEDS and CLOTHES, SILVER WATCHES, &c.

The property of Patients who have Died

in this Hospital.

⤇ The Lots may be viewed, by applying

to the STEWARD and AGENT.[18]

==

---

[18] Ibid.

==

Public Occurrences.

AN EXTRAORDINARY ATTEMPT ON THE LIFE OF BONAPARTE

The Paris Papers that arrived to the 27th, on Monday night, inform us—

On the evening of the 24th, as the Chief Consul was going to the Oratorio, an attempt was made on his life. A cart, loaded with a barrel of gunpowder, was placed in such a manner as to interrupt his passage; but the coachman drove past it exceedingly rapid. The moment afterwards it exploded, and killed five persons, besides doing great mischief to the surrounding houses. No discovery had been made of the authors of this attempt; but the Prefect of Police at Paris has published a report on a plan somewhat similar, detected two months ago, the

Conspirators in which are said to have been men implicated in the massacres of Sept. This event has been made the subject of a violent harangue in the Tribunate, which we should suppose to be directed against England, as they charge upon this Nation the Murder of Kleber, and as they assert that the same agents are concerned in the present attempt.— [*For further particular see page* 7.][19]

==

==

PAPAL BULL AGAINST PROFANE DRESSING

The importance of this object was deeply felt by Clement of Alexandria, who declares, 'that women should on no account be suffered to appear

[19] Ibid.

before men in indecent apparel, lest the latter be led into temptation, and the former themselves be drawn into unrighteousness, when they attract the eyes of the other sex.' His Holiness accordingly has briefly enjoined us to repress, by *fine* or *corporal punishment,* according to the circumstances of the case, these crying enormities: he directs too, that their punishment should be extended to such damsels as, though at first sight they appear properly attired, are nevertheless decked in *transparent* robes, and with a voluptuous and magnificent attire display themselves in very seductive and tempting attitudes. Moreover, fathers, husbands, heads of families, who weakly or negligently permit their wives, daughters, servants, &c. to trespass against these rules, shall not escape with impunity. Also, all tailors, haberdashers, milliners and men milliners, hairdressers, and others, who contribute

to these enormities of dress, shall in no wise pass unpunished.

The Bull goes on to state that "all priests, confessors, overseers, churchwardens, and others, shall in no wise admit such delinquents to the holy supper; that they shall not allow women improperly dressed to enter the church, and if they come they will be driven out; and if they resist, the higher powers shall be required to lend their aid."

This Bull is dated at Rome, the 16th of October, 1800. In reading it, the Ladies of this country, feeling the opposition to which Catholics are subject, must congratulate themselves in belonging to the *Reformed* Church, which secures not only freedom of opinion, but freedom of dress![20]

==

---

[20] Ibid.

=====================================

TO THE UNFORTUNATE AFFLICTED WITH A CERTAIN DISORDER,

THE PROPRIETOR of the ANTI-VENEREAL DROPS earnestly recommends the early use of them.

The superior efficacy of the above Drops can be attested by thousands, as they cure, in the shortest space of time, without confinement or hindrance of Diet; in general, one or two Bottles is sufficient for the cure.

CASE I. —JOHN GAGE, of the Strand, London, was afflicted five years with a Venereal Complaint, and suffered through every stage of the disease. He was a length so extremely emaciated, from the repeated mercurial frictions he had undergone, and from the virulence of the

disease, that he despaired of ever getting a cure: a dreadful sore Throat, with Nodes and Ulcers over almost every part of his Body, was among some of the complaints he suffered. At length, he was recommended to make trial of the Drops; on taking the two first Bottles he experienced considerable relief, the ulcers in the throat began to heal, he had better nights and gained strength and spirits; by persevering in the use of the Drops a few weeks he was perfectly cured.

CASE II. —ANN JOHNSTON, of First-street, Soho, London, unfortunately contracted the Venereal Disease; after undergoing two salivations, and her constitution being greatly impaired, she was advised by a Friend to make trial of the Anti-Venereal Drops, which in a short time relieved and at length perfectly cured her.

⇰ Numerous Cases of a similar kind may be published, did the limits of a Newspaper admit.

The above Drops may be had of Mr. Mottley, Grande Parade, Portsmouth; Mr. Watts, Gosport; Mr. Dimmock, Winchester.[21]

===

===

TO THE ASTHMATIC and CONSUMPTIVE

and those affected with

COUGHS and COLDS

MR. CUNDELL most respectfully informs the Nobility, Gentry, and the Public in general, of the unprecedented Cures effected through the Administration of his IMPROVED BALSAM of HONEY, which must have afford a happy sensation

---

[21] Ibid.

to those who have derived the benefit; and as the best recommendation to the future purchase of this Medicine, he begs leave to submit for their perusal the following Café:

MR. HENRY CUNDELL, —Sir, The very great benefit my daughter has received by the use of Cundell's Balsam of Honey, demands that I should lay before the public the situation she was in before she had recourse to it.

In the beginning of the present year she caught a violent cold, which affected her lungs for very much, that I thought it expedient to call in a medical Gentleman, who attended her for a considerable length of time; but every effort of his seemed not to have the effect of abating the continual coughing she had long laboured under, that his opinion was, "to have further advice would be only expending my money to little purpose, and

desired that I would permit her to take whatever she had an inclination for."—A particular friend of mine requested me to try your Balsam of Honey, from the benefit his family had received from it, particularly his son, who was relieved of a fever cough by the use of it. I therefore requested he would procure me two bottles of it, which he did: it was administered agreeable to the Directions, and after repeating it several times, have the pleasure to observe, that it considerably relieved her cough, caused her to expectorate a great deal of phlegm; her appetite increased, and gained strength daily, and is now able to undertake a voyage to Lisbon, where we are...

=======================================

==

BROADSTAIRS, NEAR MARGATE

JULY 19, 1800.

SIR,

FOR several years I was afflicted with Lowness of Spirit, as also with the Loss of the Use of my Limbs, my Legs were swelled to a considerable size, and my whole Nervous System was affected; I had every Medical assistance the country could afford, without receiving any benefit whatever; I had given up every hope of ever recovering my health again; but, being advised to make trial of your NERVOUS CORDIAL, of which I took several bottles, am now happy to inform you that my health is perfectly restored, and that I never experienced a better state of health than I now enjoy. The only return I can make you for the

blessings you have bestowed on me, is, that you have my permission to make this Case public.

I am, with respect,

Your grateful humble servant,

E. ATHERDEN, Baker,

Broadstairs, Kent[22]

==

James C. Mottley, Sr. and his wife, the former Hannah Earle, had eight children: Hannah; Mary; James C., Jr.; Samuel; George; Sophia; Elizabeth; and Thomas. The Mottleys lived in a comfortable home well stocked with books. One can imagine their lively evenings together, reading aloud to one another. In the days before radio, television, movies, videos and the Internet, it must have been a joy to have an attentive circle of listeners. Although their education was informal, it was probably better than most. By considering literacy a basic necessity and making

---

[22] Ibid.

fireside readings a ritual, the Mottleys must have imbued in all of their children a thirst for knowledge.

In searching for more information about James Mottley, Sr., I found in the Hampshire Record Office a James C. Mottley, Sr. document for redemption of land tax (50M63/C49/113), dated November 24, 1798, in which a redemption of £1-15-0 was paid for the year starting March 25, 1798.

"Mr James Motley"[sic] of Portsmouth paid taxes on "a free hold messuage[23] or tenement with appurtenances situate in the High Street in the borough of Portsmouth in his own occupation." Redemption was a system whereby one could pay a lump sum and be except from further annual bills. [24]

---

[23] messuage - a building or place of shelter to live in; place of residence; abode; home. http://dictionary.reference.com/browse/dwelling

[24] Reference to James Mottley at Guildhall Library in SFO/MS11936/292. Policy no 444388 Sun Fire Office.

I was also able to find information pertaining to a fire insurance policy:

> 444388m 24 June 1782, Baker.
>
> James Mottley of the High Street in the parish of Portsmouth in Hants, stationer & perfumer, on his now dwelling house only situated as aforesaid Brick & tiles, small part timber not exceeding Four hundred & Eighty pounds 480
>
> Household Goods therein only not exceeding
>
> Two hundred pounds 200
>
> Utensils & stock therein notexceeding
>
> Five hundred pounds 500
>
> Wearing apparel therein only not exceeding
>
> One hundred pounds 100
>
> Kitchen only separate Brick & tiles not exceeding
>
> Twenty pounds 20
>
> C Foules H Watts W Hamilton £1,300[25]

[25] Ibid.

From this document we learn that in 1781, James C. Mottley, Sr.'s house and his shop had an estimated value of £480 and his business, an estimated value of £1300. This is interesting, considering that the buildings were made of wood and fire engines or other methods for extinguishing fires were non-existent. The exact High Street address is not stated.

The insurance premium amount is not mentioned. "Baker" was probably simply an internal reference. The three names at the end were the appraisers.

The following are three deeds:

17M49/18

This is an indenture[26] of release, dated June 20th 1812.

[26] Indenture - a deed or agreement executed in two or more copies with edges correspondingly indented as a means of identification. 2. any deed, written contract, or sealed agreement. 3. a contract by which a person, as an apprentice, is bound to service. 4. any official or formal list, certificate, etc., authenticated for use as a voucher or the like. 5. the formal agreement between a group of bondholders and the debtor as to the terms of the debt. http://dictionary.reference.com/browse/indenture; an old-fashioned word for a contract. An agreement in writing in which the paper was torn into

Made between the following parties:

i George Mottley of Haslar near Gosport, gent,

ii Robert Boswell, late of Gosport, but now of Hardway, Alverstoke,

iii John Whitcombe of Bingham Town, Alverstoke, son of Thomas Whitcombe, late of Gosport, and

iv Samual Thomas Welch, builder of Gosport,

v James Collins, gent of Gosport

The following is from a lease and release of March 23rd & 24th 1798 made between:

i Thomas Whitcombe, late of Gosport, brandy merchant, deceased, (father of John mentioned above) & Thomas Andrew Minchin, gent

ii Robert Boswell, gent

---

two pieces, and looked literally like teeth. When the paper is torn into two pieces, each partner retains one piece, almost like a receipt, thus claiming in ownership.

iii George Mottley, gent

Lands mentioned in this document were leased to George Mottley and his heirs during the life of Robert Boswell in trust and Thomas Whitcombe & his heirs, who were to receive rents. Following death of Thomas Whitcombe (March 27, 1809), his son John put land up for sale at the "India Arms Inn" on April 16, 1812, and Samuel Thomas Welch bought it for £1,995. Payments made between the parties required information regarding the property in consideration, with a statement regarding the parties owing money, and to whom the money was owed:

> Concerns Messuage on the south side of the Middle Street, Gosport, late in the occupation of William Mondey, and garden, demised in 1806 to Thomas Whitcombe & William Mondey. The gardens, messuage and buildings are described in some detail, the land being 24ft by 30ft, plus a 9ft wide passageway to South Street.

Consideration; £1,995

Final page of the deed lists all the transactions over the land between 1668 and 1805, in total 31 feofments [sic],[27] wills, indenture & deed polls.

Signed & sealed by George Mottley, Robert Boswell & John Whitcombe

<u>Endorsements</u>

a) Receipt for £1,995 by J Whitcombe

b) Witnessed by Robert Cruickshank & Henry Neale

<u>17M49/19</u>

---

[27] Total relinquishment and transfer of all rights of ownership in land from one individual to another. A feoffment in old England was a transfer of property that gave the new owner the right to sell the land as well as the right to pass it on to his heirs. An essential element of feoffment was livery of seisin, a ceremony for transferring the possession of real property from one person to another. Feoffment is also known as enfeoffment. http://legal-dictionary.thefreedictionary.com/feoffment

This is an indenture of assignment for 1000 years dated 20th June 1812, for the same property as described above

i Cornelius Hayter, late of Gosport, now of Wickham, esq.,

ii George Mottley of Haslar, gent,

iii Robert Boswell, late of Gosport, now of Hardway, gent,

iv John Whitcombe of Bingham Town, gent, and

v Samual Thomas Welch of Gosport, builder,

vi Andrew Hewson, gent of Gosport

Messuage, workshops, outbuildings in Middle Street, Gosport, late in possession of William Monday & land attached

Signed and sealed by Cornelius Hayter, G Mottley, Robert Boswell & John Whitcombe

Witnessed by Robert Cruickshank

50M82/3u

Deed (assignment of leasehold), dated October 7th 1814 relating to the Kings Arms, Crown, Drum and Emms House, all in Petersfield.

i Joseph Eyles of Petersfield, common brewer

ii Cornthwaite John Hector of Petersfield, gent, & Thomas Belam, of Portsmouth, chymist (sic)

The previous history of these properties was as follows:

By an indenture dated July 17th 1789 William Joliffe, squire of Petersfield, devised to Edward Perryer, common brewer, certain lands, messuage and buildings lying in street leading from the Market Place to a place called Spain, abuting on the east side a messuage and garden formerly in the possession of William Pitt the elder, and a garden belonging to Adam Churcher, on the west by the property of Elizabeth Baker, widow, & Henry Budd, and to the north the garden and lands formerly belonging to Thomas Hughes, gent, and John Chitty.

By an indenture dated July 17th 1789, William Joliffe devised to Henry Coles of Hambledon, brewer, lands and buildings formerly called the Armitage, but now known as the Crown.

By an indenture dated August 30th 1796 William Joliffe devised to Henry Mullens property formerly called the Drummer Alehouse, but late the White Horse, in the street leading from Market Place to Chapel Green.

By an indenture dated August 30th 1796 William Joliffe leased to Henry Mullens land called the Braziers.

By an indenture dated October 20th 1807 Henry Mullens devised all the above properties to Joseph Eyles.

Cornthwaite John Hector and Thomas Belam buy the property from William Joseph Eyles for £2,590.

> William Joseph Eyles receives £2,590 from Cornthwaite John Hector and Thomas Belam[28]

Two other references to James Mottley, Sr., are the following:

> In 1781 James Mottley of Portsmouth had a house and shop worth £480 (GL [Guildhall Library] SFO/MS11936/292. Policy no 444388)... while Mottley's stock was worth £500.

> James Mottley, printer and bookseller 1779-1798 [sources: Hampshire Directory; Graham Pollard ed 1955; The Earliest Directory of the Book Trade by John Pendred (1785); UBD [Universal British Directory][29]

James C. Mottley, Sr. and his son, James C. Mottley, Jr., were actively involved in promoting the culture of Portsmouth at the

---

[28] Ibid.

[29] *Hampshire Papers 3- Printers, Bookseller, and Libraries in Hampshire 1750-1800*, by John Oldfield (Hampshire County Council 1993), p. 8, p. 23 (in a list of Portsmouth Printers).

end of the 18th century. Following are references regarding the Mottleys' contribution to Portsmouth culture:

> The *Hampshire Telegraph* was established in 1799 by Mr J C Mottley, and from then on a clear picture of musical activities in Portsmouth emerges. It is apparent that there was a clientele for books and sheet music in town. Mr Mottley, printer and stationer, was also a keen retailer and apart from his medicines and elixirs (which were advertised regularly), he publicized a new book that was to appear on 1 January 1800, a General Treatise on Music... written on a new plan by Mr King. Two weeks later he was offering new music by Massinghi and Reeve, the Comic Opera of Ramah Droog in Piano score 'songs sold singly', and sonatas for pianoforte, violin, flute, and violincello. [30]

---

30 https://books.google.com/books/about/Music_in_Portsmouth_1789_1842.html?id=kg0vJwAACAAJ
Music in Portsmouth 1789-1842 (Portsmouth Papers), by Frank Warren, Irwen Cockman. Publish date is December 1969, published by Portsmouth City Council. The 10 digit ISBN is 0901559970 and the 13 digit ISBN is 9780901559975. http://www.allbookstores.co.uk/book/0901559970/Music_in_Portsmouth_1789-1842_Portsmouth_papers.html

Apparently, James, Sr. and Jr. sold tickets for local concerts at their store. One of the concerts, held in the Crown Inn on April 14, 1794, consisted of two works by Handel, with the second half of the concert in honor of Franz Josef Haydn, who visited the city that year. A violin concerto was performed by the leader Mr. Mountain:

> A violin concerto was performed by Mr Mountain, the leader of the orchestra... Tickets on this occasion were 4s each and were available at Mr Mottley's stationary shop in Portsmouth...[31]

Like his father, James C. Mottley, Jr., the eldest son, was an expert businessman. Under his management, the printing, publishing and bookstore businesses continued to flourish. James, Jr. also expanded the stationer's business to include the sale of other products. The store advertised an assortment of elixirs and preparations for treating a large variety of ailments. James, Jr. was also involved in real estate and other business

[31] Ibid.

dealings with his younger brother, George, and his brother-in-law, Thomas Belam.

As stated in the *Portsmouth Telegraph* article, in 1800, the Mottleys published *A General Treatise on Music*, by M. P. King. Two weeks later, the store featured new music by Massinghi and Reeve, *The Comic Opera Of Ramaah Droog* in piano score, "songs sold singly," and sonatas for pianoforte, violin, flute and violin cello.[32]

The poet Samuel Taylor Coleridge (1772 –1834) was a guest of James C. Mottley, Sr., whom he described as a prominent resident and bookseller. Coleridge confided to his friend William Wordsworth in code how appalled he was by Mottley's personal habits: smoking, drinking and his ability to swear like a sailor, and what he described as his addiction to sleeping with women of all classes, in spite of having a lovely wife and six or seven children.

[32] Op. Cit., *Music in Portsmouth 1789-1842*

On Monday, March 4, 1805, James C. Mottley, Sr.'s obituary appeared in the *Portsmouth Telegraph:*

> This evening, at six o'clock, died, after an illness of two months, which he bore with the most Christian fortitude, Mr Mottley, sen, in the 68th year of his age. He will be long lamented by his afflicted family. [33]

George Mottley, Mary Mottley's Father (1776-1840)

George Mottley was born in May 1776, the third son of Mr. James C. Mottley and his wife, Hannah. He was baptized at St. Thomas church in Portsmouth October 14, 1776.

George was one of eight children born to James and Hannah. As so often happens in families, some individuals by their very personalities, talents, ambition and accomplishments leave more lasting memories. Three members of this family, James, Samuel and Elizabeth, were integrally involved in Mary's life.

[33] The *Portsmouth Telegraph* Monday, March 4, 1805, page 3, col. 4.

Mary Martin Mottley, Mary Mottley's Mother (1774-1840)

The Martins were an old Hampshire family that lived in Hambledon, located ten miles north of Portsmouth. Hambledon dates back to Saxon times and was at the crossroads of several important events in English history. During the English Civil War (1642-51) and following his defeat at the Battle of Worcester, King Charles II sought shelter in a house in the village of Hambledon before fleeing to France.

Hambeldon was known for its vineyards. It is recorded as being the first commercial vineyard in England since the dissolution of the Monasteries by Henry VIII. It was also referred to as the "cradle of cricket," since this is where the game originated. It is thought that the Hambledon Cricket Club was founded about 1750.

For several generations the Martins were butchers. Mary Martin's mother (Mary Mottley's maternal grandmother), Mary Childe from Alverstoke, married Thomas Martin when still a minor, with written permission from her father, Richard Childe.

The affidavit states that Mary was fully consenting to the marriage. By an odd coincidence, Mary Childe's new husband, Thomas Martin, was also a butcher like her father, Richard Childe. One can be sure that both of these families always had a plentiful supply of meat on their tables! Two children were born to the couple, Mary Martin and Thomas Martin, Jr.

On April 9, 1785, George Mottley married a young lady named Mary Martin from Hambledon. He was 19 and she was 22. In January of1795 they moved into the officers' quarters of the

Royal Hospital Haslar where George held the managerial position of agent until he retired in 1833.[34] A hospital agent received upper-mid level grade of pay at three hundred pounds per annum. He had a number of important responsibilities that included management of finances, supplies, hospital staff, and safety of patients' belongings. An intelligent, educated man, apparently George was an excellent bookkeeper.

---

[34] In 2009, Haslar Hospital closed permanently, with plans for the government to convert it into a Veterans Care Village. - email from E Birbeck, Hampshire, England, sent July 29, 2009.
"After campaigning against the closing of Haslar, disgruntled local people pointed out that Britain became one of the only Western nations not to have a dedicated military hospital. Since the Ministery of Defence sale of site there are now plans to turn the it into a retirement home with leisure facilities for former UK military personnel."http://www.dailymail.co.uk/news/article-2426569/Inside-Britain-s-naval-hospital-Georgian-building-fully-equipped-latest-medical-equipment-FOUR-YEARS.html#ixzz3pDKXQDMu

Royal Hospital Haslar – Door to George Mottley's Office

Royal Hospital Haslar

Since George had to rely on the "ward nurses" of the time, his work must have been frustrating and hazardous. "Nurse" was certainly a loose term when describing 19th century hospital caregivers. Nursing schools did not yet exist, so to find qualified women who would make suitable nurses must have been a challenge.

In *A History of Haslar,* W. Tait writes: "the agent explains that the whole amount of the effects of people who die in the hospital, is what he receives from "the nurses who attend the party in his sickness, which cannot be depended upon."[35]

In *The London: The first hundred years, 1740-1840,* a study of the voluntary hospital system in England, Dr. Clark- Kennedy offers insight regarding the evolving nursing profession.[36] Describing the dilemma of finding suitable staff at the London in the early 1700s, Dr. Kennedy writes:

---

35 http://www.jameslindlibrary.org/articles/the-royal-hospital-haslar-from-lind-to-the-21st-century/

36 London pride: the story of a voluntary hospital, by Archibald Edmund Clark-Kennedy, Hutchinson Benham, 1979 (Original from the University of California Digitized Sep 16, 2011), https://books.google.com/books/about/London_pride.html?id=MPBQAQAAIAAJ

> A major problem was finding the right women to nurse the patients. The sisters of the pre-reformation hospitals had disappeared at the Dissolution of the monasteries during Henry VIII's reign. Nursing had not yet been rediscovered as a vocation for women. So they were compelled to recruit for this purpose, without asking too many questions. Often the women were elderly. Some were respectable widows but others of doubtful past and uncertain sobriety and who could no longer earn a living other ways were employed. Nevertheless, rather surprisingly, most could write, or at least sign their names; nor is it right to write off the nurses of those days as a wholly bad lot.[37]

At Haslar it was the policy of the Commissioners of the sick and wounded that all patient effects should be entered into a book on admission to the hospital. In spite of their insistence that this policy be followed, no record of such a book exists.

---

[37] Ibid.

All of the other records kept so methodically by George Mottley are impressive for their detail. If handwriting delivers important clues about the character of a person, George Mottley was a man well worth knowing. Evidence from original archived records bearing his flamboyant, beautifully scripted signature indicates that he was a conscientious person who expertly conducted his administrative duties.

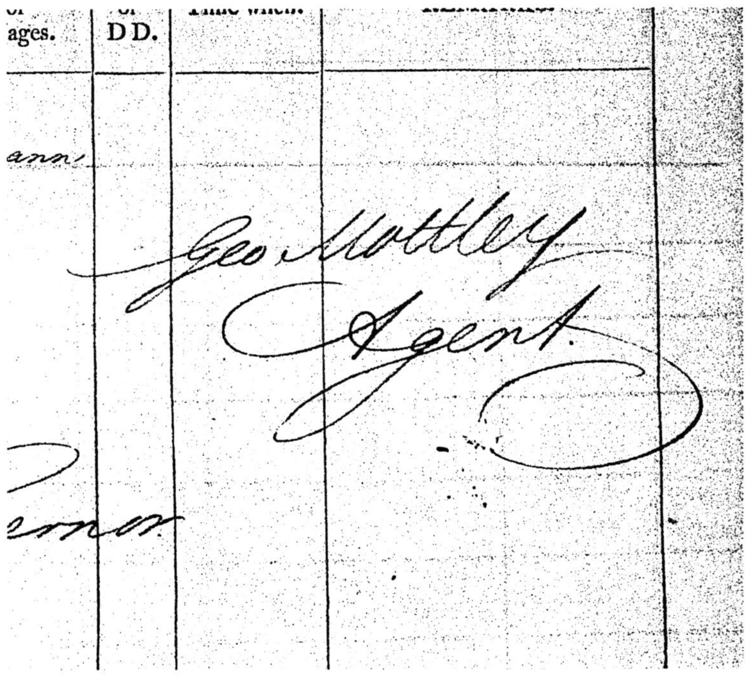

George Mottley's Signature

One has the impression that he was a loyal part of the management team, deeply attached to his colleagues at Haslar. Soon he became an assistant to agent John Newsham in proving patients' wills. Eventually he assumed Newsham's position and launched his own distinguished career at Haslar.

In addition to being a hospital administrator, George Mottley was also an investor who partnered with his brother-in-law, Thomas Belam, who was married to George's sister Elizabeth, in many business ventures.

In 1833, after serving as agent at Haslar for 38 years, George was transferred to the Royal Naval Hospital in Stonehouse, located in the county of Devon near the port of Plymouth. It is unclear whether this relocation was by his request or whether it was part of the hospital system's routine procedure. Apparently this is where the family was living in 1835, because it is known that during that year Alexis de Tocqueville traveled to Devon to meet the Mottley family and ask for Mary's hand in marriage.

George Mottley remembered all of his children in his will, including his daughter Mary, who at that time was already Mme. Marie de Tocqueville.[38]

The Mottleys were known as a close-knit, hard-working, innovative family, many of whom are remembered even today as prominent members of their community. Several of the sons rose in the ranks of the Royal Navy or played a large part in the success of the emerging bourgeois class.

Mary Martin apparently was proud of the Martin family legacy, since four of their children were given the name "Martin" as their middle or second name. Eventually Mary Martin and George Mottley became the parents of thirteen children, of which Mme.

---

[38] Op. Cit., material provided via the services of Anthony Adolph, Genealogist, www.anthonyadolph.co.uk, and can be verified via hard copy, dated November 12, 2001, as filed in the archives of Sheila Le Sueur.

de Tocqueville (Mary Mottley), born on August 20, 1799, was the eldest daughter.

The Mary Martin & George Mottley Children

Of the Mottley sons, Samuel Mottley rose to the rank of Rear Admiral in the Royal Navy. In 1763 he married Ann Price. They had four daughters and a son, whose names were Mary, Eliza, William, Ann and Jane. Unfortunately, the family was plagued with infant and early childhood mortality. Only the last two daughters survived: Ann, born October 10, 1794; and Jane, born December 29, 1806.

Many years later, Ann and Jane were plaintiffs in a lawsuit in Chancery. Their uncle, Thomas Belam, made provisions for his property and insurance policy with Equitable Assurance, London, naming his brothers-in-law, Rear Admiral Samuel Motley and George Mottley, agent of the Royal Hospital Haslar, as his trustees and executors.

The youngest Mottley son, Thomas, was born in 1771. On March 13, 1807, he married Mary Corrie and they had four children: Georgina, born May 1808; Augusta Martin Mottley; Henry Hood North Mottley; and Hewson Harrison. Hewson and Hood were also employed by the Navy, suggesting that Thomas, who worked for Customs, was well connected with Naval administration and was able to secure good positions for his sons.

In the early 19th century, Mary Martin Mottley's home town of Hambledon suffered a setback when members of the population joined the migration to Portsmouth, seeking work and better opportunities. Although Mary Martin was now living with her husband, George, in Alverstoke, she maintained a close relationship with her family. During one of her visits to Hambledon in 1803, their second daughter, Louisa Eleanor, was born.

By the time George Mottley died, he had already retired from his position at the Royal Naval Hospital in Stonehouse, Devon. His obituary appeared in the *Gentlemen's Magazine*: "April 10 1840 at Stonehouse, age 73, George Motley, Esq. late agent of the Royal Naval Hospital at Haslar."[39]

Probate was granted to George's oldest living son, Thomas Martin Mottley. It was fitting that Thomas should be the executor of his father's will. He was "the good son." An honest man and a captain in the army, it was customary not to marry until well after thirty years of age. Thomas remained a bachelor and was "holder of the purse" for the family. Mary Mottley was always included as one of the beneficiaries, even when she was married and had been living in France for many years.

Mary Martin Mottley outlived her husband George by several years and died at the age of 89. The cause of her death was registered as dysentery, an illness that is treatable today. At the

---

[39] Ibid.

time she died she was living in the home which her son Thomas Martin Mottley had purchased for her at # 2 Grove Road in the district known as Cams.

Seven of Mary Martin Mottley's 13 children preceded her in death. When she passed away, three of her daughters, all on their forties, were living with her: Louisa Eleanor, now a widow; Elizabeth Martin Mottley, listed as a spinster; and Margaret Claributt Mottley, also unmarried. Margaret was given the middle name of Claributt after a surgeon, Dr. Claributt, whom her father admired at Haslar. [40]

Since middle class women were classified as one level above working class girls who went into service as maids and housekeepers, they were condemned to a life of good works and embroidery. Life for them must have been totally frustrating. The Mottley family is reminiscent of those described in Jane Austin's novels.

---

[40] Ibid.

Mary Martin Mottley seemed to be an excellent household manager. As the mother of 13 children, this was probably out of necessity. The older children were probably well-trained to look after the younger ones, although the family also had several servants. In her will Mary Martin Mottley left firm instructions that provided for her servants a month after her death, thus allowing them sufficient time to find other employment. One of the servants, Mary Walch, whom she must have trusted, witnessed the codicil to her will.

One has a sense that George and Mary Martin Mottley married for love and the two enjoyed a happy life together. Several of the sons rose in the ranks of the Royal Navy. Of the 13 children, only one of them, their son, Joseph, a Rear Admiral in the Royal Navy, produced a grandchild, Arthur.

The Mottley lineage ended in 1947, when another Mary Mottley, Arthur's widow (Mme. de Tocqueville's nephew), passed away, leaving no heirs.[41]

Mary Mottley's Earlier Years

On March 2, 1801, Reverand John Hall baptized Mary and her older brother Thomas, at St. Mary's Church in Alverstoke in Hampshire County, where the hospital was located.

In addition to her Aunt Elizabeth and Uncle Thomas Belam, two other uncles, her father's brothers, James and Samuel, also played a prominent role in Mary's upbringing.

Although she was the eldest girl born to George and Mary Martin Mottley, Mary had two older brothers, Roger and Thomas. Roger died in April, 1802 at age six. Other Mottley siblings were: George, Jr., born in 1801; Joseph, born in 1802; Louisa Eleanor, born in 1803; Elizabeth, born in 1804; Carolyn, (Catherine Ann),

---

[41] Ibid.

born in 1805; James Charles, born in 1810; Margaret Claributt, born in 1811; Anna, born in 1813; Catherine, born in 1814, and Henry Bayless, born in 1816.

Mary's sisters, Anna and Caroline, died within a year of their birth. Roger, the Mottleys' eldest child, died at Haslar Hospital in 1802, only six years old. As soon as they became adults, Mary's other brothers established their own professional careers.

It is believed that Mary went to live with her Aunt Elizabeth Mottley and Uncle Thomas Belam, her father's sister and brother-in-law, in Petersfield, Hampshire around 1804, when she was approximately four years old.[42]

Petersfield served as a post for the London-Portsmouth stagecoach, so it was undoubtedly an excellent location for serving Thomas Belam's business interests. A prosperous merchant, Thomas owned several enterprises. By profession he

[42] Ibid.

was a druggist, a chemist and an apothecary.[43] Apothecaries were well respected for their contributions to health care. Thomas was also an assistant surgeon, with the added responsibility of teaching surgeons.

Unlike physicians, surgeons were not educated in universities or medical school and they were not entitled to be addressed as "Doctor." In fact, even in the 21st century, surgeons in the UK, although university educated, are referred to as "Mr." This information is confirmed by George Wilson Pierson in his book, *Tocqueville in America,* where Pierson describes Elizabeth Belam as "being an undistinguished woman who was said to be the widow of a Portsmouth pharmacist."[44] Pierson makes no mention of Thomas Belam's surgical profession, indicating its relatively insignificant value.

---

[43] A druggist; a pharmacist. http://dictionary.reference.com/browse/apothecary.

[44] http://www.amazon.com/Tocqueville-America-George-Wilson-Pierson/dp/0801855063

Thomas Belam owned a house in the High Street of Portsmouth at White Hart Row and a cottage with a beautiful garden in Chalton, in addition to his primary residence in Petersfield. He also owned or was part owner of several breweries in the Petersfield area. Thomas worked closely with his brother in-law, James C. Mottley, Jr., advertising his remedies in the *Portsmouth Telegraph* and selling them in the Mottleys' shop.

An example of one of Thomas's products for which I found an advertisement in the *Portsmouth Telegraph* and *Naval and Military Journal, Volume 1 January and February,* was the "Balm of Gilead," a cordial that was said to "be peculiarly adapted to the female constitution." It was effective for "phlegmatic habits, a weak stomach and the nervous system," and "wonderfully suited for recovering the tone of the urinary and genital organs."

The "Balm of Gilead" was also said to be "effective for men and it would contribute more safely and honorably to conjugal happiness." The "Balm of Gilead" was derived from a tree known as Balsam of Gilead. The botanical name is *Commiphora*.[45]

By popular demand, James and Thomas sold a book (two volumes for the price of one) titled *A Guide to Old Age; Or Cure for the Indiscretions of Youth,* by Dr. Brodum. Dr. Brodum was a scoundrel and was later arrested.

==

Just Published, Price Three Shillings and Six-pence, with the Doctor's Portrait, dedicated to the

KING'S MOST EXCELLENT MAGESTY,

A New Edition, in German and English, of an entire New Work, entitled,

A GUIDE TO OLD AGE; or, A CURE for the INDISCRETIONS of YOUTH.

To which he claims the attention of all Parents, Guardians, &c. whole duty it is to

[45] The Archive of Britain.

pay special regard to the interests of the rising generations. Neither single or married should be without it, and in particular seafaring men on long voyages; in which the various disorders incident to mankind, and particularly those occasioned by irregular propensities in both sexes, with the proper mode of relief, &c. are treated of under the following heads: —

Nervous disorders, head-ach, epilepsy, madness, deafness, diseases of the eye, consumptions, atrophy, or nervous consumption, jaundice, bilious complaints, complaints of the female sex, diseases of the head, diseases of the liver, asthmas, dropsy, gout, rheumatism, palsy, menstruation, chlorosis, scrosula, excess of the libidinous indulgences, baneful effects of such indiscretions, especially among youth, venereal disease, on sea and hot bathing.

By WILLIAM BODIUM, M.D. LONDON.

Printed for the Author, and sold at his House, No. 9, Albion-Street, near the Leverian Museum, Blackfriarsbridge; sold also by J.C. Mottley and W. Donaldson, Portsmouth; and maybe had of all the Booksellers and Venders of the Dr.'s Medicines in the three kingdoms.

The high estimation in which this Work is held by the public, its great utility, and the unprecedented sale it has met with, is fully proved by the following testimony:—

"I do certify, that I have printed Thirty Thousand of Dr. Brodum's Guide to Old Age, since the first Publication."

J.W. MYERS, Printer[46]

==

[46] Ibid.

No doubt Thomas Belam and James Mottley sold the "medicines" in good faith. But there is a deeper meaning when one stops to consider the plight of sick people at that time. Clearly they were suffering, so it was easy for them to ignore the possibility that these medicines were effective therapy for the multitude of diagnoses listed. Amazingly, some people were helped; the remedies may have served as placebos.

One can surmise that Mary was a bright child and possibly the Mottleys saw a larger future for their eldest daughter by giving her the opportunity to be raised by the Belams. Undoubtedly the Belam household must have been a sanctuary for Mary, if only to escape from the bedlam in her own home. The Belams had no children of their own and from the day Elizabeth, a favorite sister and aunt, started to care for four-year-old Mary, she became Mary's mother. Perhaps the only reason Thomas and

Elizabeth Belam did not adopt her was because the practice of formal adoption did not exist until 1926.[47]

The only mention of Mary's real parents was upon the occasion of her wedding when both her mother and father were recorded as attending the ceremony. According to custom, her father, George Mottley, gave her away.[48]

In addition to offering Mary Mottley love and security, the Belams also provided her with financial opportunities that may not have been available to her had she remained in Devon with her family. Mary was probably mostly self-taught. One book with which she was familiar that was a part of the Belams' library was *Bailey's Dictionary.*[49] If Mary's reading list had been limited

---

[47] The adoption system was not placed in England until 1926 due to the law that only biological heirs could own property previously owned by parents. https://prezi.com/zzmbwi73v9hh/history-of-adoption/

[48] Op. Cit., material provided via the services of Anthony Adolph.

[49] Nathan Bailey's 'Dictionarium Britannicum' was first published in 1730. It contains 48,000 words. Bailey's dictionaries were extremely popular: they were larger and more comprehensive than any other dictionaries of the day, and they also sold more copies. Samuel Johnson owned a copy which he scribbled over, underlining sections and adding his own ideas. It would later

to this single book, she would have been well educated. The *Dictionary* is an amazing compilation of valuable information and was highly revered by writers and wordsmiths. It is said that Samuel Johnson's copy was well marked up.

Mary was apparently an avid reader who was fluent in German and Italian as well as English. Even though occasions for expressing her views would have been rare outside of home and hearth, one could surmise that Mary didn't hesitate to speak up whenever she did have the opportunity. Through Alexis's correspondence to Mary and trusted colleagues who recognized Mary's intelligence, it is clear that the two thrived on their lively conversations.

In 1815 when Mary was 16, once again her life changed radically. Thomas Belam died prematurely at the age of 39 and was buried April 3, 1815. The cause of death on the certificate was "a tired

help him to write his own dictionary. http://www.bl.uk/learning/langlit/dic/bailey/1730bailey.html

body."[50] Thomas appointed his brothers-in-law, Samuel Mottley and George Mottley, to be his trustees and named his wife as residuary legatee.

Judging from his last will, Thomas Belam must have been a very generous person. In addition to providing an annuity for his parents, he cancelled the £300 debt he had advanced to them for a mortgage on their house in Sussex. He also ensured that his business interests would continue after his demise.[51]

Thomas Belam bequeathed £1,000 to Mary Mottley upon her 21st birthday, or married with her father's permission. Mary also received a cottage with a garden in Chalton.[52]

Shortly after her husband's death, Elizabeth Belam moved to France and settled outside of Paris in Versailles. Apparently it

---

[50] Op. Cit., material provided via the services of Anthony Adolph.

[51] Ibid.

[52] Ibid.

cost less to live in France at that time, so many English people relocated. Mary accompanied her aunt, and although from time to time they returned to England to visit the family, for the most part they remained in France. Throughout her life Mary was attentive to her aunt's needs. They enjoyed a warm mother-daughter relationship.

As Mary grew older, even though she still resided with her aunt in Versailles, it has been suggested that she worked as a governante (housekeeper) for an aristocratic family, but there is no firm evidence to prove that fact.

Retracing Mary's Steps

Each of my "Mary Mottley Pilgrimages" to the UK and France seemed to bring me closer to Mary, the Mottley family, and then later to her life with Alexis in France.

4

Who was Alexis de Tocqueville?

Portrait of Alexis de Tocqueville

Politics in 18th & 19th Century France

As landowners the French aristocracy had the benefit of living a life of leisure. Property and other assets were passed down from one generation to the next. They also derived a steady income from taxes collected from the peasants who lived on and worked the land of their vast estates.

To protect this feudal Master-Slave system, the aristocracy also supported the belief that they were descended from an elitist bloodline. Their "birthright" gave them privileged status, delivering the perception of being rightfully set apart from the commoners or the masses. Examples of caste systems were prevalent not only in Europe but also throughout the world since the beginning of human history.

Since the French aristocracy also subscribed to the belief in Divine Right of their ruler, they were closely linked to the Roman Catholic Church, which in turn leaned on royalty and the Throne for its financial sustenance. This closed circle of codependency was effective as long as the bourgeoisie and peasants remained ignorant and illiterate. It would only be a matter of time, however, before the carefully protected myths of a "royal bloodline" and "Divine Right" were exposed.

Slowly the commoners were waking up. As the bourgeoisie grew wealthier and more educated, they started to question church authority. They also resented outright the privileged lifestyle of the aristocracy. Even large sums of money couldn't buy titles and bloodlines.

Ultimately the middle and lower classes came to realize that as long as they subscribed to the belief that they had no free will and could never escape from the class into which they had been born, the aristocracy would continue to keep them enslaved. Revolution was in the air.

At the end of the 1700s, France was on the brink of bankruptcy. King Louis XVI's[53] lavish spending, financial support of the American Revolution, 20 years of drought and cattle disease resulting in heavy taxes, led to peasant and urban uprisings among the poor. Rioting, looting and workers' strikes set the stage for revolution.

In 1786 when Louis XVI's controller general Charles Alexandre de Calonne proposed a financial reform package from which the privileged classes would no longer be exempt, trouble was already brewing. The king needed support for this radical reform, so for the first time since 1614, the king called for a May 5, 1789 meeting of the Estates-General, an assembly representing France's three Estates: the Clergy, Nobility and Middle Class. In the interim before the meeting, delegates from the Three Estates were charged to compile lists of grievances which they would present to the king.

---

[53] King Louis XVI reigned from 1754-1793

Although 98 percent of the Third Estate of France's population was now middle class—a radical change from 1614—they could still be outvoted by the Nobility and Clergy. It was time for reforms. The Third Estate started to rally for equal representation and removal of the Nobility's veto power. By June 17, 1789, the voting process had become the major issue, overshadowing the original purpose of the meeting. The Third Estate met alone and took on the title of National Assembly. Three days later they met and took the Tennis Court Oath, vowing not to disperse until they had achieved constitutional reform.

On June 27, with most of the clerical deputies and 47 liberal nobles joining the middle class, Louis XVI was forced to reform the Three Estates into a new assembly. The peasants ran amok, looting and burning the homes of tax collectors, landlords and other overlords. The French nobility, seeing the handwriting on the wall, started to flee to neighboring aristocratic countries.

Then on July 14, 1789, rioters besieged the Bastille fortress in an attempt to secure gunpowder and weapons. This event, known as The Storming of the Bastille, is considered by many to be the start of the French Revolution.

On August 4, 1789, when the National Constituent Assembly abolished feudalism with the signature of the Declaration of the Rights of Man, historian Georges Lefebvre later called this event the "death certificate of the old order."[54]

The constitution that was formally adopted on September 3, 1791, however, was hardly a fair and just representation of the middle class. Essentially it established a constitutional monarchy. The king retained veto power and could appoint ministers. Maximilian de Robespierre (1758-1794), Camille Desmoulins (1760-1794) and Georges Danton (1759-1794) called for a more republican form of government and the trial of Louis XVI.

---

54 http://www.history.com/topics/french-revolution

On August 10, 1792, extremist Jacobins arrested Louis XVI, initiating yet another countrywide massacre. The National Convention replaced the Legislative Assembly, proclaiming the abolition of the monarchy and establishment of the French Republic. On January 21, 1793 King Louis XVI was condemned to death for high treason and crimes against the state and sent to the guillotine. His wife Marie-Antoinette (1755-1793) was beheaded nine months later.

In June 1793, the Jacobins seized control of the National Convention from the more moderate Girondins, established a new calendar and dispensed with Christianity. Thus began the 10-month Reign of Terror ("la Terreur").

On March 12, 1793, only three months before the beginning of the Reign of Terror, Louise Madelaine Le Peletier de Rosanbo married Hervé de Tocqueville at Malesherbes where the young couple lived until the Committee of Public Safety arrested her entire family. Louise Madeleine, 21 at the time, witnessed the condemnation to death of her grandfather, Chrétien de Malesherbes, both of her parents, her elder sister and her husband of the Chateaubriand family. It is said that she was permanently traumatized by this experience.

Under the direction of Robespierre, it is estimated that over 50,000 suspected enemies of the Revolution were guillotined during the Reign of Terror. On July 28, 1794, the madness ended when Robespierre himself was executed.

On August 22, 1795, only 10 years before Alexis's birth, the National Convention passed a new constitution that created France's first two-party legislature. Parliament appointed a five-member Directory to serve as Executive power.

A chaotic four years followed in which General Napoleon Bonaparte (1769-1821), the new commander of the army, quelled one uprising after another until, on November 7, 1799, Bonaparte staged a coup d'état, abolished the Directory and in 1804 (a year before Alexis de Tocqueville was born) appointed himself France's "first consul." Thus began the Napoleonic Era in which the general waged wars against several European coalitions and expanded his empire.

In 1812, however, Napoleon was forced to abdicate the throne after an unsuccessful invasion of Russia. Although in 1815 he returned to power again and waged his famous Hundred Days Campaign, Napoleon experienced a crushing defeat at the Battle of Waterloo. He was exiled to the island of Saint Helena, where he died at age 51.[55]

Even if the Congress of Vienna set out to restore Europe to pre-French Revolution days, the aristocracy must have already known this would be impossible. The country had been profoundly impacted by the Revolution and Napoleonic reforms.

---

[55] http://www.history.com/topics/napoleon

Napoleon had reversed some of the most radical religious policies of the Convention and in 1804 had established the Civil Code, which recognized political and legal equality of all adult men. He replaced entitlement by birth and social standing with a meritocracy. Based on their talents and skills, the people could now earn the right to be educated or employed. This was a major reform that could not be retracted without yet another revolt.

If Alexis Charles Henri Clérel de Tocqueville, born on July 29, 1805, had come into this world at any other time than directly following the French Revolution and a year after Napoleon Bonaparte's coup d'etat, perhaps we would say that as a member of the nobility he was among the more fortunate. Yet ironically it is exactly because he *was* a member of the nobility during this chaotic period in French history, that he had plenty of fertile material for dedicating his life to social and political criticism of his own class.

It was the Era of Enlightenment both in America and Europe. Popular sovereignty and inalienable rights—individualism, the general will, French philosopher Roussseau's social contract, and Baron de Montesquieu's doctrine regarding of the separation of powers—were the backbones of both the French and American Revolutions. The two countries' declarations, delivered within 13 years of each other, bear the stamp of a shared philosophy and authorship.

Basic concepts contained in the 1989 Declaration of Man are derived directly and in some paragraphs almost verbatim from America's Bill of Rights and Declaration of Independence. These concepts are the foundation for the philosophical doctrine of Enlightenment: individualism, the general will, the social contract as theorized by Rousseau, and the separation of powers espoused by Montesquieu.

At the time of the French Declaration, Thomas Jefferson was in France serving as a US diplomat. Jefferson worked closely with Gilbert du Motier, Marquis de Lafayette, the main sponsor of the Declaration of the Rights of Man. Like Jefferson, Lafayette embraced Enlightenment doctrines of constitutionalism, popular sovereignty and natural rights.[56]

It was revolutionary to consider that "men are born and remain free and equal in rights, and that "social distinctions may be founded only upon the general good." The notion of natural rights to property, liberty and life were heady and empowering. Moreover, *it was not the role of government to control and manipulate the people, but to recognize and secure their free and natural rights.* Everywhere, change was in the air. It was an exciting time to be alive.

---

[56] http://alphahistory.com/frenchrevolution/declaration-rights-of-man-and-citizen/#sthash.FXZJGTdP.dpuf

Alexis's Early Years

Alexis de Tocqueville's pedigree was impeccable. He was the youngest of three sons born to Hervé Louis François Jean Bonaventure Clérel de Tocqueville (Compte de Tocqueville, 1772-1886), a Norman nobleman, and Louise Madeleine Le Peletier de Rosanbo, descended on her mother's side from Vauban and Chrétien-Guillaume Lamoignon de Malesherbes, a famous lawyer and royal administrator who became Alexis's role model.[57] Through her father, Louise belonged to the Rosanbo family. Louis le Peletier de Rosanbo was president for life of the Paris Parliament.

---

[57] Chrétien Guillaume de Lamoignon de Malesherbes, (born Dec. 6, 1721, Paris—died April 22, 1794, Paris), lawyer and royal administrator who attempted, with limited success, to introduce reforms into France's autocratic regime during the reigns of Kings Louis XV (ruled 1715–74) and Louis XVI (ruled 1774–92). When his father became chancellor of France under Louis XV in 1750, Malesherbes was appointed president of the Cour des Aides in Paris and directeur de la librairie (director of the press), the chief censor of published material. The latter office, which he held until 1763, gave him the authority to allow the philosophes (writers of the Enlightenment) to publish many of their works. In particular, most of the volumes of Denis Diderot's Encyclopédie, which adopted a skeptical attitude toward Roman Catholic and feudal institutions, were published during this period. http://www.britannica.com/biography/Chretien-Guillaume-de-Lamoignon-de-Malesherbes

Early Years – Abbé Le Sueur, Alexis's Beloved Tutor/ Surrogate Father

Alexis was a sickly child and often lonely, since his older brothers left home to join the military. His mother's failing health caused her to withdraw from family activities, so she was hardly a companion, and his father was often away, attending to his responsibilities as a prefect or magistrate. His tutor, Abbé Le Sueur, a kind and gentle man, became the most stable presence in the young boy's life.

The priest already had a long history as a Tocqueville family tutor and was much beloved by Alexis's parents and grandparents. In 1778 he first joined the family as a tutor for Hervé, Alexis's father. Hervé's parents were warm and caring people who were stalwart members of the Norman nobility during the Ancien Regime. It is believed that Abbé Le Sueur came from Picardy, but his name "Le Sueur" is of Norman origin and once belonged to the noble families in the area. Perhaps Picardy was the location of the religious order of which he was a member.

The Catholic Church as the First Estate at that time in France was a powerful force. It is unlikely that Abbé Le Sueuer was a parish priest. Rather, it suggests that he also came from a noble family and filled the traditional role of being a tutor and caregiver to the children of the noblesse. He later became what is known as a non-juring priest. This meant he refused to take the oath to support the revolutionary constitution, thus making him a marked man. As unrest grew among the French people, ultimately deteriorating into an uprising in 1792, he was forced to flee from Paris and return to Picardy.

After Hervé de Tocqueville was married and had his own family, Abbé Le Sueuer returned to the Tocqueville family and once more resumed his role as tutor, this time to the young Tocqueville sons, Hippolyte, Edouard and Alexis. He taught the boys ethical and moral values and introduced them to their religion. Alexis loved his tutor like a father and sometimes took advantage of his "Bebe," who spoiled him almost as a loving grandparent.

In 1820 when it was time for Alexis's formal education, he moved to his father's home in Metz and was enrolled as a student at the Lycée. The good Bebe was saddened at being separated from his favorite pupil, but understood it was time for Alexis to move on to more advanced studies. The tutor had fulfilled his work; he had instructed his young pupil in the art of rhetoric and French literature. He had also ensured that his young charge was given the foundation for a sound religious education.

Abbé Le Sueur wrote a letter to Alexis, instructing him to be civil with all of his comrades, thus preparing for some of the pitfalls he might encounter at the Lycée. He also warned Alexis not to form any special friendships with them. It was believed that the Abbé was referring to homosexual friendships, which apparently were common in Lycées.

Alexis never demonstrated the least interest in such a relationship, but he did form a lasting friendship with a fellow student, Eugene Stoffles. Eugene was a member of the bourgeois community in Metz and as one would suspect, this didn't seemed to bother Alexis. Throughout his life, he never made a serious decision without consulting Eugene. Alexis was godfather to Eugene's son, also named Alexis, and was influential in the young man's life.

Alexis's cousin, Louis de Kergolay, was also a close confidant. Louis's father was Cesar de Kergolay and his mother was Blanche de la Luzernen, the daughter of Alexis's grandfather Malesherbe's nephew. Louise de Tocqueville and Blanche de Kergolay were cousins and Louis was born in 1804, one year before Alexis. The cousins remained close friends throughout their lives.

Abbé Le Sueur felt that Louis de Kergolay was a bad influence on Alexis. Some years earlier, Kergolay had suggested that Alexis should choose a military career. The Abbé protested it would be a great shame to put such a head under a helmet, and resolved to "request Monsieur Loulou to mind his own business."

Abbé Le Sueur was probably in his early sixties when he began to tutor the Tocqueville sons. It is a certainty that he loathed those of a liberal persuasion. In 1822 is the following excerpt from a piece he wrote:

> All of Europe is infected with this cursed race... Ways must be invented to stop the contagion. There ought to be a leper house in the frozen seas of Siberia where the sowers of the plague

> would be shut up; there they would be subject to quarantine lasting not for days but for years. I am convinced that none of them would ever return.[58]

In his biography of Alexis de Tocqueville, Andre Jardin suggests that the piece was deliberately outrageous to amuse the person to whom it was addressed. It may have been written to provide insight into the inevitable signs of democracy, freedom and equality influencing French politics.[59]

Abbé Le Sueur remained with the Tocqueville family for the rest of his life. In 1831 when Alexis and Gustave de Beaumont were preparing to leave on their voyage to America, Alexis left with the blessings of his beloved "Bebe." By this time, Alexis had already shown signs of distancing himself from his Catholic faith. The priest, now in his eighties, feared he would not live to see Alexis return. Alexis for his part tried to hide his religious

[58] Jardin, Andre; Deva, Lydia; Hemenway, Robert. *Tocqueville: A Biography.* New York: Macmillan, 1989, p. 43.

[59] Ibid.

differences from his old friend for fear of hurting someone he loved so deeply.

While he was living with his father in Metz, Alexis started to question Catholic doctrine and his religious upbringing. Hervé was often away while attending to his work for the prefecture. During those times, Alexis enjoyed browsing in his father's library, soon discovering the works of Voltaire, Montesquieu and Rousseau. The writings of these men opened Alexis to enlightened ideas that resonated with his deepest convictions about the sovereignty of man and caused him to critically examine the catechism.

Andre Jardin suggests it was the influence of these works that first ignited the idea that a democratic world might one day replace the aristocratic one. Even though it countered everything his class believed in, the ideas of these enlightened intellectuals became the foundation for Alexis's writings.

For the most part Alexis accepted the fact of a Supreme Being and that there was life after death. In a letter to Alexis, Louis de Kergolay poses questions to him about his faith:

> Here you're reverting to a fault that I've always seen in you… which is to give too much consideration to the opinions of a mass of men… will you believe a foolish unbeliever more than Christians or your Bebe, whose opinions you and I flatly condemn in private?[60]

Although Alexis may have had doubts regarding his faith, there is no evidence that he tried to deceive his old friend.

Abbé Le Sueur was unaware of Alexis's fears until 1824 when he learned that he had failed to make his Easter duty. Alexis wrote back that although he was a believer, he could not be a practicing Catholic.

---

[60] Op. Cit., Jardin, Andre. *Tocqueville: A Biography*, p. 63.

Alexis and Abbé Le Sueur maintained a frequent correspondence. His old friend had a refreshing sense of humor combined with a seriousness that was always gentle.

When the time came for Alexis to depart for America, Bebe presented him with a book of prayer as a farewell gift. Although he knew Alexis had become influenced by non-Catholics, he believed that deep down his student had a religious and good nature. He also knew they would never meet again on this earth. The Abbé inscribed the sign of the cross on the front leaf followed by these words:

> We are nearing, my friend, the moment of your departure. The unhappy circumstances in which we find ourselves require this painful separation, which is going to cost us many tears, especially as I may not hope for more than a few days longer on earth. I should be inconsolable if, on bidding you goodbye,

> I said to myself: it is for always! But no, dear friend, you shall follow me there where, by the grace of God I hope to go...
>
> The sky is the goal toward which we are both tending. I have well studied the road; and as we cannot travel together, and as I should arrive well before you at the rendezvous, I am going to briefly trace the path for you. I shall indicate the provisions to be made for the journey and the encounters to be avoided... Faith... Hope... Charity... Truth... Patience... Then the things to be avoided.... Pride... Incontinence... The Philosophers... finally the close:
>
> Adieu once more. I commit you and your kind companion to the care of Divine Providence. My wishes, my prayers and my blessings will go with you, everywhere.[61]

In failing health herself, Louise de Tocqueville lovingly cared for the good priest and family friend during his last illness. Alexis

[61] Pierson, George Wilson. *Tocqueville in America.* JHU Press, 1930, p. 37.

received the news of his passing in a letter waiting for him when he arrived in Boston. He was so deeply grieved it was two weeks before he was able to share his loss with Beaumont.

Brokenhearted, Alexis wrote to his brother Edouard, the only person whom he felt would truly understand his grief:

> I felt... the most lively and painfully sharp grief I have ever felt in my life... I loved our good old friend as I loved our father; he always shared our concerns, our worries, our affections, and yet nothing tied him to us but his own wish... There is no getting accustomed to the idea of having the support of one's childhood, the friend (and what a friend!) of one's whole life disappear just like that... a man whose thought, every affection turned on us alone; who seemed to live on us alone; who seemed to lie only for us.... I have lost one of the greatest goods of this world. Ten years may pass and this will be just as true as today. The more I compare his friendship for us with

> everything else I know of the same kind, the more I find that it was like nothing else in the world, and yet now it is nothing more than memory.[62]

Alexis must have been well versed in French history, particularly the Revolution and Napoleonic Era. Had the Reign of Terror not left an indelible mark on his immediate family? Unlike his aristocratic relatives who refused to remove their blinders for fear of exposing themselves to a vulnerability they were too frightened to confront, at a certain point in his academic studies, Alexis started to develop a questioning mind.

The spirit of the Enlightenment was contagious. The narrow carefully guarded parameters of his childhood had already started to expand as soon as he left home and was given the key to the "candy store," his father's library in Metz. One can imagine Alexis's excitement and enthusiasm as he started to explore the works of Thomas Hobbes, John Locke, François-Marie Arouet

[62] Op. Cit., Jardin, Andre. *Tocqueville: A Biography*, p. 40.

(Voltaire), Baron de Montesquieu, Denis Diderot, Jean Jacques Rousseau, Thomas Hobbes, Benjamin Franklin, and Thomas Jefferson.

Alexis realized he could no longer accept any ideology at face value. Every doctrine he had ever been taught needed to be carefully examined from the perspective of each of the great philosophers and social critics of the time. Only then would he allow himself to form his own opinions.

With this changed attitude toward the aristocracy and French politics, it is not surprising that Alexis would have stepped out of his rank and file in order to court a woman who was neither an aristocrat nor a Catholic. Both were merely labels as far as he was concerned. Fervently he embraced the idea of a meritocracy that distinguished an individual not by pedigree or pocketbook, but by intelligence, character, personal accomplishment, wit and verve.

Thus, in spite of the Tocqueville biographers who deliberately slighted Mary Mottley, one could assume that this young opinionated woman was totally aligned with Alexis's enlightened humanism.

Louis Edourd de Tocqueville (1800-1874)

Edouard, the second son of Count Herve de Tocqueville and his wife Louise, was described by George Wilson Pierson as "of becoming a cultured and conservative seigneur, a fit scion of his life."[63] Edouard fulfilled that role admirably.

Following the fall of Napoleon and accession of King Louis XVIII, young men from the noble families rushed to join the King's guard. Edouard and his older brother Hippolyte were among them. Edouard eventually was forced to resign for health reasons; he had developed rheumatoid arthritis. He was depressed and no doubt in pain for several years.

[63] Op. Cit., Pierson, George Wilson. *Tocqueville in America*, p. 17.

In 1826, after Alexis completed his law studies, Edouard, restless and free from the army, accompanied Alexis on what might be regarded as a "right of passage" for that time. Both of them enjoyed traveling and in December they set off on a tour of Italy and Sicily, returning to France in April 1827.

On this journey Alexis recorded everything he felt, saw and experienced. In museums he missed nothing; he looked at every painting carefully, writing about each work in great detail. It was a memorable trip for both young men.

In 1829, Edouard married Alexandrine Olivier, and from all accounts this proved to be a happy union. Alexandrine came from a rich bourgeois background; both of her parents were well placed and accepted in Parisian society. Through the marriage Edouard become one of two hundred of the largest shareholders in the Bank of France. He also became the manager of Baugy, a large agricultural estate in the Oise section north of Paris.

The family lived in the Baugy Château surrounded by acres of parkland. Edouard and Alexandrine had two boys and three girls. The present family is descended from their second son, Hubert.

Edouard had other abilities besides farming; he was also interested in economics. Alexis is known to have teased him for being thrifty. Social problems and the challenge of dealing with pauperism and customs regulations suggest that if only by default, Edouard would have also been open to considering democratic ideas. He is the author of a published work on the agricultural economy and he also collaborated on a work titled *Les Annales de la Charite.*

Edouard was interested in the environment and considered natural laws basic to a sound agricultural economy. A sincere and thoughtful man, Edouard was also dedicated to preserving Christian principles in the society of the day. He and Alexandrine made sure their children were educated in Catholic schools and raised in a Christian home.

Alexis was a frequent visitor to Baugy. An indulgent uncle to their children, he was godfather to their eldest son, Hubert. Edouard and Alexandrine set aside a room for him in their home, providing him with a peaceful place to write. It was here where he began to write *Democracy in America.* In 1835, Alexis and Mary spent the first few months of their marriage at Baugy with Edouard and Alexandrine.

In 1852, Alexis's political views conflicted with his brother's when Edouard ran for the Legislative Assembly. Although Edouard denied it, Alexis feared his brother's actions would be interpreted as his own and this would have an adverse effect on him politically. Edouard was defeated in the election, which partially helped to heal the rift. The disagreement was severe and both brothers suffered and were saddened by it. Thereafter they carefully avoided political discussions.

Far more damaging to their relationship was Alexis's marriage to Mary. Edouard once described the family feelings toward the union as being those of resignation. They didn't hesitate to voice their opinion of Mary as a difficult character with a fiery temper. After their father Count Hervé died, the relationship became more distant. However, when Alexis was critically ill and dying from tuberculosis, both Edouard and Hubert were at his bedside.

Hippolyte de Tocqueville

On the *Tocqueville Culture – France* website one finds the following biography of Hippolyte de Tocqueville:

> Hippolyte, the eldest child of the Clérel de Tocqueville family, was born on October 1, 1797. At the fall of the First Empire, he decided to pursue a military career. Along with his father, he

joined the King's Guards on July 1, 1814, and remained in the army throughout the Restoration. He resigned on October 15, 1830, after having refused to swear an oath to the new regime, and never, despite several attempts, was able to rejoin. From this moment on, he devoted himself to his new domain, the Château de Nacqueville, of which he had become the owner through his marriage to Émilie Evrard de Belisle de Saint-Rémy in 1826. He also nourished political ambitions, but these were sustained only by his extremely volatile convictions and patent opportunism: in 1833, as an impassioned legitimist, he published Lettres aux Normands, in which he expressed his horror of the triumph of the bourgeoisie and the middle ground under the July Monarchy. This, however, did not keep him from turning republican in 1848, and swerving resolutely to the left when he was elected, with the help of his brother Alexis, conseiller général of the department of La Manche.

"My poor Hippolyte, what poor character, but what a heart of gold!" wrote Alexis in a letter to Gustave de Beaumont. (February 3, 1859)

After the events of December 2, 1851 and the reestablishment of the Empire, he aligned himself with the new power, and openly took Edouard's side in his quarrel with Alexis over the attitude they should adopt towards the new regime. This last about-face ended up exasperating Alexis de Tocqueville, who by then was accustomed to being criticized for his brother's political antics. All of these political differences did not, however, completely estrange the two brothers, and Alexis was profoundly touched, for example, to see Hippolyte at his bedside during his last winter at Cannes. [64]

Curiously, in another book about the Tocquevilles is the following:

---

[64] http://www.tocqueville.culture.fr/en/portraits/p_famille-hippo.html

> Secretly accompanying Tocqueville to America was his brother, Hippolyte. In December of 1831, the two accidently separated, never to see each other again. Alexis returned to France and fame as a world renowned social commentator, Hippolyte stayed on in America and accomplished even more in his own way. [65]

In 2006 I visited the Château de Nacqueville, which is now maintained by Florence d'Harcourt and her family. A distant Tocqueville relative, Florence, her husband and children were living in Australia when they were contacted by the Tocqueville family, inviting them to move into the Château and help with its renovation.

The following is a description of the Château de Nacqueville:

---

[65] *Hippolyte: Little Known Facts About Alexis de Tocqueville's Lesser Known Brother*, by Ken Hinrichs http://www.amazon.com/Hippolyte-Little-Alexis-Tocquevilles-Brother/dp/1475989830

Of the three north Cotentin houses that were divided between Hippolyte, Édouard and Alexis de Tocqueville, the Château de Nacqueville is the only one that had not been owned by the Clérel de Tocqueville family. The Château, which dated back to the 16th century, was inherited in 1822 by Émilie Erard de Belisle de Saint-Rémy, the future wife of Hippolyte de Tocqueville. It had undergone a number of modifications since its construction, but what changed its appearance the most was the demolition of the very high wall that had, until 1700, enclosed the manor house. Today, all that remains is the postern opposite the main building. After 1700, it was possible to plant gardens around the house, but it took until 1830 and the arrival of Hippolyte de Tocqueville for the necessary work to be carried out. It should be emphasized that at that time, the lanes that led to the Château were still barely passable, and that the lack of upkeep of the grounds had turned them, in the eyes of Alexis, into a huge "quagmire."

Nevertheless, at the instigation of Hippolyte, a radical transformation took place. His interest in gardens and botany (which most of his family shared) were a help to him in this. He was also aided by an English landscape architect, who designed a romantic park that extended across all three of the small valleys that converged on the Château, and that cleverly made use of the small streams that ran down them. The road that led to the estate was redrawn so that it ended right at the main house, the garden was planted with many flowering shrubs and exotic plants, and a pond was dug downstream from the Château in the direction of the sea, which could be seen on the horizon. The streams were turned into cascades of water that enlivened the masses of flowers, and a number of fountains were added to the gardens.

The Château itself was not spared this prodigious energy: the roof was raised to allow another floor to be added, and the interior was greatly improved, which elicited the admiration of Alexis de Tocqueville every time he paid a visit to Nacqueville.

Although it suffered a great deal of damage in the 20th century due to various storms as well as the Second World War - during which it became a favorite location for American army headquarters - the park at Nacqueville was restored to its 19th century glory, and even today it remains one of the most sumptuous gardens in this part of France. [66]

[66] http://www.tocqueville.culture.fr/en/lieux/l_chat-nacqueville.html

5

Marie & Alexis

We will never know if it was coincidence or destiny that brought Alexis de Tocqueville and Mary Mottley together under circumstances that gave them a chance to get to know each other, but what we can say with certainty is that the meeting was never intended to be merely a passing moment in either of their lives. In the eyes of family, friends and possibly everyone except Mary's guardians, the Belams, and Alexis's closest friends, Gustave de Beaumont and Ernest de Chabrol, everything was wrong about Mary and Alexis as a couple. Perhaps that is exactly why Alexis and Mary knew from the start that they were right for each other.

Even after the relationship had begun, if Alexis had chosen to terminate it, Mary, as a woman and commoner, would have had to resign herself to his decision. Under ordinary circumstances, Alexis was a man who was out of her league.

Yet these two people continued to confirm to each other and to the outside world that they had little regard for pedigrees and pocketbooks when used as a measuring rod of a person's character or worth.

Both Alexis and Mary were products of changing times, with education as the spoiler or catalyst. It must have become self-evident to each of them even before they met that if not for ignorance, fear and the stranglehold of the Church and Crown, feudalism would have been abolished long ago.

After attending college in Metz at age 18, Alexis began his studies in law at the Royal College Paris. Simultaneously, in 1826,

Alexis's father, Hervé Louis François Jean Bonaventure Clérel de Tocqueville, became prefect of Versailles, the most influential prefecture in France.

In 1828, Alexis, now a jurist and two fellow jurors, Gustave de Beaumont and Ernest de Chabrol, rented a house near the Belam residence in Versailles, where Mary had already been living since she was sixteen. As neighbors, eventually they met.

Mary was an intelligent, well-educated woman who now spoke fluent French in addition to her native English, German and Italian. Even though formal education was not yet permitted for women and certainly not for commoners, she was an avid reader.

Alexis soon became a frequent visitor at the Belam home. He must have found Mary to be a woman of many interests, one of which was politics. He began to share with her his belief that democracy would inevitably find its way into the life and government of France. One imagines that Mary was an eager participant in evening fireside conversations with Alexis and his colleagues.

Alexis had such a great admiration for Mary's intelligence and keen perception, eventually he grew to depend on her feedback for all of his written work before releasing it to a publisher. A more serious relationship started to blossom between the two as they continued to spend more time together.

Unquestionably theirs was a romantic union. Otherwise, the two would not have put each other through the pain and suffering caused by a socially mismatched marriage. Alexis ignored the gossip and did as he pleased. He felt he had found his intellectual match in Mary and he also felt she would provide stability for his high-strung impetuous nature. He was devoted to her.

The July Revolution of 1830 that put the "citizen king" Louis-Philippe of Orléans on the throne was a turning point for Alexis. It deepened his conviction that France was moving rapidly toward complete social equality. Breaking with the older liberal generation, he no longer compared France with the English constitutional monarchy. Now he looked toward democratic America for his role model. Of more personal concern, despite his oath of loyalty to the new monarch, his position had become precarious because of his family ties with the ousted Bourbon king.

Alexis and Gustav de Beaumont, seeking to escape from their uncomfortable political situation, asked for and received official permission to study the problem of prison reforms in America. They also hoped to return with knowledge of a society that would mark them as especially fit to help mold France's political future.[67]

---

[67] http://www.britannica.com/biography/Alexis-de-Tocqueville

By steamboat, stagecoach, on horseback and in canoes, Tocqueville and Beaumont traveled for nine months visiting America's penitentiaries along much of the East Coast and then traveling as far west as Michigan. In Pennsylvania, Tocqueville spent a week interviewing every prisoner in the Eastern State Penitentiary. In Washington DC, he called on President Andrew Jackson during visiting hours.

When learning about Alexis's visit to America and his growing passion for enlightened humanism and a democratic way of life, it was Alexis's visit to a Pennsylvania prison that first captured my attention. The purpose of visiting American penitentiaries was to confirm that the success stories touted by those who were responsible for this new type of penal system were actually true.

One can only imagine how the prisoners must have felt when this stranger with a foreign accent came to their cells to question them. They had no idea the young man was an aristocrat from

France. Responding willingly to his questions, Alexis must have realized this may have been the first time in their entire lives that anyone had shown any genuine interest in their feelings and thoughts. Suddenly they were recognized as human beings with a mind, a heart and families whom they may never see again.

This human interaction set Alexis apart from others of his class as well as from the social norms of the time. Although he was unable to offer the prisoners hope, he freely gave them the gift of himself.

This is the man who married Mary Mottley against the wishes of his family, the norms of his class, against all odds—and who remained devoted to her throughout their married life.

By the time Alexis departed for America in 1831 with Beaumont, Mary and Alexis had probably already started to talk about marriage. In one of Alexis's letters to Mary, written in July of

1932, Alexis exclaimed: "Oh that is your great talent, Mary: you always reconcile me with the world and with myself."[68]

One imagines that Mary was very supportive of Alexis's journeys abroad. The two must have carried on a copious correspondence during the time they were apart. Alexis would have discussed many of his observations, conversations, and speculations that paved the way for his prodigious study of American culture that led to the writing of *Democracy in America.* Mary's comments would have been rich with her own reflections and thoughtful insights. In Mary Alexis found a woman who was both intelligent and articulate.

The differences between the backgrounds of the two were so pronounced, it was almost as if nature had placed before them every possible impediment just to test their mettle. Was this love, or just a passing fancy? Could the relationship withstand the hostility and pressure from family, friends and colleagues?

---

68 http://www.tocqueville.culture.fr/en/portraits/p_mottley-02.html

One of the biggest disputes among historians when discussing Mary Mottley is whether she should be faulted most for being five years and eleven months (or was it a full nine years, as some historians claim) older than Alexis. The issue of age difference was more related to child-bearing than anything else. It must be remembered that at that time woman's greatest attribute was considered her ability to have children. The older a woman became, the less capable she would be of bringing forth a (male) legacy.

It is recorded that Alexis discussed his forthcoming marriage to Mary with his sister-in-law Emilie. The conversation suggests that he had doubts about choosing Mary as his wife. A better interpretation might have been that his only doubt was that by marrying out of his class, he knew he would hurt his family.

It is said that of the many titled families in France, if asked to choose one that would be more liberal or open to accepting a commoner in their midst, surely the Tocquevilles would have been high on the list. As landlords they were known to be well respected by their tenants and servants whom they treated with kindness and respect. Yet apparently when the issues were closer to home, i.e., when family members were expected to warmly welcome commoners like Mary Mottley into their inner circle, they could be as arrogant and snooty as the rest of their aristocratic friends.

Nevertheless, Alexis didn't give anyone much choice. He made it clear that he wasn't interested in marrying a young girl whom he didn't know. He believed he would "only find happiness in union with a wife who would merge her existence with his, and who would entirely unite her life to his tastes and convictions of the world."[69]

---

[69] Tocqueville, Alexis de. *Memoir, Letters and Remains.* Ticknor and Fields, 1862, p. 45.

Either they accepted the English commoner Mary Mottley as his wife, or they didn't. Their opinions didn't seem to matter to either Alexis or Mary. Alexis wanted Mary as his wife and he would have her as his wife, and that was that.

In the spring of 1835 while Alexis de Tocqueville was on a visit to England, he made a point of visiting the Mottley family in Devon. The purpose of the visit was two-fold: to introduce himself to the Mottley family and to ask for Mary's hand in marriage.

To resolve one of the major differences, Mary was apparently willing to concede on one account. Before becoming Madame Marie de Tocqueville, she converted to Catholicism. As for the rest of the differences, time would be the ultimate judge. And so it was. Against the wishes of the entire de Tocqueville family, the two were married at St. Thomas d' Aquinas church in Paris on October 25, 1835.

Only the principal witnesses were listed in the marriage certificate, so it is unclear if any of Mary's brothers and sisters attended the wedding.

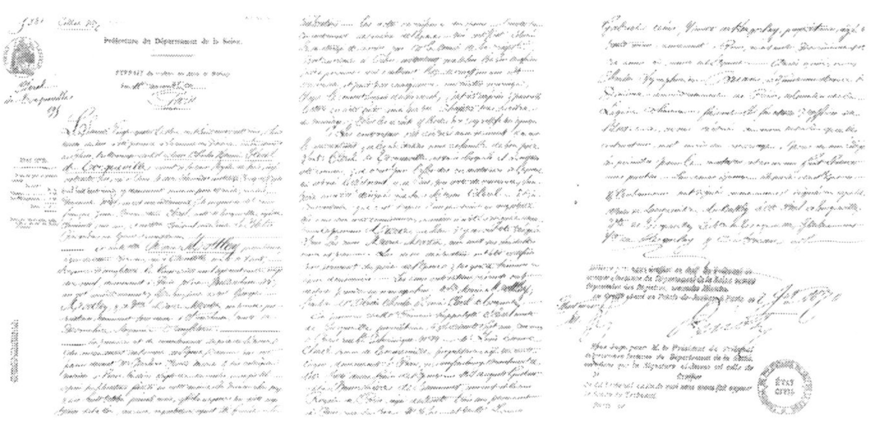

Marriage Certificate of Mary Mottley and Alexis de Tocqueville

Curiously, Mary's date of birth was incorrect in the civil register and also on the marriage certificate at St. Thomas Aquinas church. No one seemed particularly concerned about correcting it. It was enough that she was "older," so it seemed hardly necessary to set the records straight.

Surely Mary's aunt, Elizabeth Belam, would have been one of the honored guests, although her name is not on the list. Mary Mottley's parents must have felt highly uncomfortable and very much out of their realm. George Mottley would not have enjoyed the hostility from Mary's future in-laws as he gave his daughter away during the ceremony. Well aware that his daughter was a "cause célèbre" in Parisian society, it wasn't easy for a man of considerable standing in his own community to witness his daughter treated like a pariah.

With her usual aplomb and outspoken disdain for society, Mary must have weathered the storm by ignoring the snubs altogether. She had no use for Parisian salon society. Alexis and books were her companions.

Alexis's mother, Louise, was unable to attend the wedding ceremony. Rumors flew that her absence indicated her disapproval, but apparently this was untrue. At the time Louise was seriously ill and she died at her home three months later. Alexis mentions Mary's sorrow on learning the news of his mother's death because Louise had been kind to Mary.

Apparently Alexis felt his mother would have done everything possible to put Mary at ease. She had suffered immense tragedy in her life and surely would have been sensitive to others' pain. Also, was she not devoted to Alexis, and did she not want him to be happy?

Although the wedding was hardly another military battle of the same proportion as the Battle of Trafalgar which Lord Nelson's Portsmouth flagship, *HMS Victory,* waged against the French in 1805, for those who stubbornly drew a line in the sand between titled landowners and commoners, it might as well have been. The 25-year-old memory of that famous battle in which the

French were defeated was still raw; after all, it was the decisive one that ended the Napoleonic Wars.[70]

From the moment their vows were pronounced until the moment of their parting at death—and maybe after that, who knows?—the marriage was strong.

In an August 5, 1836 letter written to his cousin and lifelong friend, Count Louis de Kergorlay, Alexis wrote:

> I cannot tell you the inexpressible charm which I found in living so continually with Marie, nor the treasures that I was perpetually discovering in her heart. You know that in travelling, still more than at other times, my temper is uneven, irritable and impatient. I scolded her frequently and almost always unjustly, and on each occasion I discovered in her inexhaustible springs of tenderness and indulgence; and then

[70] War of the Third Coalition (August–December 1805) of the Napoleonic Wars (1803–1815).

I cannot describe to you the happiness yielded in the long run by the habitual society of a woman in whose soul all that is good in your own is reflected naturally, and even improved.

When I say or do a thing which seems to me to be perfectly right, I read immediately in Marie's countenance an expression of proud satisfaction which elevates me. And so when my conscience reproaches me her face instantly clouds over. Although I have great power over her mind, I see with pleasure that she awes me; and as long as I love her as I now do, I am sure that I shall never allow myself to be drawn into anything wrong.

You asked me, my dear friend, to speak of myself and of Marie; I have opened to you my whole heart. There is one idea connected with this subject which often troubles me. You will soon be married, and I cannot help trembling lest the kind and friendly relations that would be so favourable to our intimacy

> should not be established between our wives; for experience will teach you how difficult it is to separate oneself in any way from one's partner.
>
> In this respect Beaumont's recent marriage is sure to be very agreeable to me. I see that a real friendship is likely to spring up between Marie and Madame de Beaumont, and from that minute our intimacy will be secure for the rest of our lives. Take notice that I speak of intimacy not of friendship, which can be affected by no external circumstances.[71]

Life after Marriage

Alexis's and Mary's first residence after marriage was the home of Alexis's brother, Edouard, and his wife, Alexandrine. This was not the happiest arrangement; it was clear to Mary that she wasn't welcome in the Tocqueville family. Fortunately the period of awkwardness and discomfort was short-lived since Alexis's

[71] Op. Cit., Tocqueville, Alexis de. *Memoirs – Letters & Remains*, p. 309.

mother Louise died in January, 1836 and Alexis inherited his grandmother's Château in the village of Tocqueville in Normandy.

It must have been a great relief for both Mary and Alexis to finally have privacy and physical separation from the Tocqueville family. It was also a perfect place for Alexis to write the second part of *Democracy in America.* He was happy to place Mary in charge of renovating both the property and grounds while he could retire to his study to spend long hours writing.

The Château, which had been vacant for fifty years, was steeped in a long and memorable history. Alexis's ancestors traced back to Guillaume Clérel, who accompanied William the Conquerer to England in the year 1066 and fought with him at the Battle of Hastings.[72]

---

[72] http://chateaudetocqueville.com/en/the-castle/alexis-de-tocquevile-and-the-chateau-de-tocqueville/

"There (at the Château)," he wrote, "I glimpse into a world of dreams. Do you know that, from the top of the tower, I can see the port where William the Conqueror embarked for his conquest of England, and do you know that all these places around me bear names that are famous in our history?"[73]

It was close enough to the English Channel for a view of the coastline from the tower. Nearby was the port of Barfleur, where Sir Thomas Becket stayed on his way from England to the Continent. In 1345, Edward III's troops landed in Normandy not far from Saint-Vaast-La-Hougue, which marked the beginning of the Hundred Years' War and where the King knighted his son, the Black Prince.[74]

Château de Tocqueville had its own mystique. There was "a certain delight in treading upon the land where one's forefathers used to live and in living among people whose origins are bound

---

[73] Ibid.

[74] Ibid.

up with our own.... I like this place," Alexis wrote in 1836. "I am going to lead an extremely orderly, tranquil life here."[75]

Mary knew how to make a home. Her first task after moving in was to create a space for Alexis as a study, to protect him from the chaos of renovation. She had soon transformed the Château into a warm and comfortable residence.

Mary and Alexis converted the fields into meadows and designed the 14-acre park into an English style garden, with a small lake and broad lawns. They enjoyed walking together under the ancient oaks and willows.[76]

The two spent their evenings in the drawing room sitting in front of a blazing fire. Alexis would share with Mary his latest pages of writing, often interrupted by animated discussions about a

---

[75] Ibid.

[76] http://chateaudetocqueville.com/en/rent-the-pavillon-de-tocqueville/the-park/.

meeting Alexis may have just had, or a book they were reading together.

Often present was one of Alexis's close friends, Jean-Jacques Ampère. Ampère, the only son of physicist, Andre-Marie Ampère (the word "amps" was derived from the family name), was a French philologist and man of letters who had also visited America.

Mary spent most of her time at the Château. She loved the Norman countryside and was kept busy supervising new repairs and generally taking care of all administrative duties. On one occasion when she discharged an employee, Alexis believed her decision was too severe. It is doubtful he would have been able to take such an action himself. Confrontation would have been too painful for him.

Since one of his major concerns was finding a solution to poverty, as a landowner Alexis wanted to set an example. Every week the staff would bake bread for the poor and Alexis and Mary would personally visit the sick.

Within the walls of their Château, the couple created an idyllic life for themselves, reading, writing, tending the property and enjoying long hours of conversation.

We can assume that most of what was written about Alexis's marriage would be negative, since the press was controlled by the aristocracy or the wealthy bourgeoisie. Also, because women were considered insignificant, Mary's name would not appear in articles written by social and political analysts. To the outside world, she was a "non-person."

Alexis and Mary were married for 24 years. It was a successful union and true partnership. Alexis respected women and Mary was in many ways his soulmate. Some have written that Mary was the motherly type and at times this was what Alexis needed. One could argue, what man doesn't want and need someone to tenderly look after him? Likewise, what woman doesn't want and need someone to care for with them and give them the same attention? Mary was Alexis's anchor and point of stability and Alexis freely admitted this.

The correspondence we have translated in chapter 9 quashes any doubts once and for all about the nature of their relationship. These letters are reminiscent of *The Letters of Robert Browning and Elizabeth Barret Browning*[77] or *The Love Letters of Abelard and Elouise.*[78] Alexis and Mary were deeply devoted to each other.

---

[77] http://www.gutenberg.org/files/16182/16182-h/16182-h.htm.

[78] http://www.gutenberg.org/files/35977/35977-h/35977-h.htm.

6

Château de Tocqueville

In the year 2000, my sister Anne and I visited our native Island of Jersey, where I had a book signing for my recently published book, *Two Flags, One Heart,* about growing up in Jersey and living through the Occupation.[79]

Afterward we took the ferry to St. Malo. Our friends, Janet and George Gaudin, met us and drove us to Coutainville to the home of friends, where we stayed overnight. The next day we set off for Tocqueville and the Château de Tocqueville.

---

[79] *Two Flags, One Heart*, by Sheila Le Sueur, Jersey: Starlight Publishing, 2000.

The Château de Tocqueville

Located in the heart of Normandy (20 km east of Cherbourg and 4 km from the sea), the Château was built in the 16th century and originally consisted of only a large Normand stone house with two towers. Buildings during the Middle Ages were constructed of wood and thatch, so the fact that it was a stone house indicates that it was a "manor" that was built for noblemen or landowners as a "stronghold." One sees evidence of this in the stone banner around the dovecote. The lord of this manor was a local justice or justice of peace.

A third tower, located at the border of the courtyard accessible by a porch, was used as a dovecote. Around 1840 when the interior of the manor was enlarged, the porch was transferred stone by stone to the middle of the driveway.

Record of the Clérels in Normandy dates back to the 16th century. In 1661 in an exchange of estates, the Clérel family acquired the manor, which was already known as "Tocqueville Manor," and added their family name to the name of the fief.

Thus, the manor became known as the Clérel de Tocqueville. Likewise, "Tocqueville" was also added to the Clérel family name, indicating the name of their fiefdom.[80] Since that time the Château de Tocqueville has remained Tocqueville property.

The manor became transformed into a castle or château in the 18th century, when the Tocquevilles married into families well-connected to the royal court. In 1896, Count Christian de Tocqueville, the great-grandfather of the actual owner, built the square tower, the Tower wing, on the southern side of the building, as well as the two annexes to the side houses.

The château managed to escape the French Revolution unscathed since the family maintained an excellent relationship with the villagers. Apparently they found no reason to upset their own security by attacking the château.

---

[80] Fief – 1. a fee or feud held of a feudal lord; a tenure of land subject to feudal obligations. a territory held in fee. 3.fiefdom. http://dictionary.reference.com/browse/fief

The last occupant of the Château was Alexis's grandmother. After she died, the Château was vacant for fifty years. Alexis and Mary must have been blissfully happy there, renovating the property and maintaining it as their own private "fiefdom."

The château miraculously survived World War II, even though The Germans occupied the area and Normandy was an active war zone. The only memento they left behind was a pair of blockhouses in the park. Novelist Ernest Hemingway, a war correspondent during the Second World War, arrived with the American troops directly after D-Day and stayed at the château.[81]

Currently residing in the Château are Tocqueville descendants, the Count and Countess de Tocqueville d'Hérouville and their children. The Count is a member of the New York and Paris Bar, who now practices law in Paris after having lived in Washington

---

[81] http://chateaudetocqueville.com/en/the-castle/history/

DC and New York City. The Count is also a founding member of the United Way in France.[82]

In 2007, I wrote a letter to Mary that mentioned my visit to the Château. Here is that letter:

> Dear Madame de Tocqueville,
>
> Yesterday I learned some interesting information, which I hope will please you and make you feel proud. Earlier I mentioned that I have not been on my "Mary" search alone. Hundreds of friends and acquaintances have joined me in my search for you.
>
> One of these persons is a true "Normand," born and bred in Granville. His name

[82] http://chateaudetocqueville.com/en/the-castle/

is Professor Jean-Louis Benoît. He is a historian and a recognized authority on "all things Tocquevillian."

Someone else I would like to introduce to you is a Jersey man named George Gaudin. George and I are distantly related. In fact it was George who took me to visit Château Tocqueville for the first time, in 2000. My sister Anne and I were visiting friends in Coutainville and we traveled to the Château in his motorcar. A ferry service between Granville and Jersey operates daily during the summer months.

The news I want to share with you is that just ten days ago a new ferryboat was launched into service. Madame, the ferry is named *TOCQUEVILLE!!* So the next time I visit Granville I will travel on the *Tocqueville!*

I can imagine how surprised both you and your husband would have been to learn about this honor. In 2007 the Tocqueville name is very present not only in Normandy and France but the entire world!

I sense a question in your eyes when I mentioned a "motor car." *What is that?* you must be asking.

Transportation has changed since your time. Horse-drawn stagecoaches disappeared long ago and no one travels on horseback except for pleasure. History tells us that you were frightened by the horses. We also know that coach drivers and even members of the aristocracy were renowned "whips," driving "to an inch," fast and dangerous!! Perhaps you had such an experience?

I live in Arizona now, in the southwest part of America. It is land that was acquired from Mexico in 1853, became a territory in 1863 and a State in 1912. This is a long way of explaining to you that I and other passengers fly like a bird, in an airplane (flying machine). It is operated by a pilot and a crew of stewards, who care for the passengers. It is possible to travel by air to London, England or Paris, France in a matter of hours! Even more astonishing is the fact that an American has even flown to and walked on the moon!

But let me bring you back to earth. A motorcar evolved from the carriages with which you are familiar, and they are immensely more comfortable. History tells us that you were afflicted with arthritis. I cringe when I think of you riding in a coach without springs or rubber on the wheels.

I mentioned that you are my teacher. Searching for you has forced me to ask questions. How, I wonder, do I describe a car, such a common mode of travel? When were they invented, and who built them?

I learned the following.

In the past, traveling from one place to another meant that one walked or used a coach. The village of Tocqueville was within walking distance from the Château but if you needed to travel farther, a coach was your only option. In the 17th century, this was by necessity the vehicle of choice, since there was nothing else except riding horseback... or on elephants, camels, donkeys, mules or other animals suitable for carrying weight on their backs. As you know, often members of the lower classes transported people on their backs. You will be familiar with sedan chairs.

But I think you and I can agree the thought of elephants at the Château presents an amusing spectacle!

The stables at the Château still stand and are in good repair. Automobiles (motor cars) have replaced the horses and carriages and there are no more coachmen. The stables are now used as "garages"—the modern version of coach houses—for the cars.

Paris can be reached in a few hours. There is no need for travelers to find lodging overnight. For longer distances the modern day traveler will rent a room in a "motel," a clever combination of the words "motor" and "hotel."

A motel consists of a bedroom with an attached bathroom. The car is conveniently parked outside. There is a main office and lounge where one registers, and often a restaurant is attached. If not, there are many other choices known as "fast food places" in the surrounding vicinity. They are much more convenient and comfortable than coaching inns with which you would have been familiar. Also, there are no "bugs" in the beds.

I'm sure you want to know the origin of the automobile, a word derived from two Latin words meaning "to move on its own." A Frenchman, Eduardo Delmare-Debouteville filed some patents for such a self-propelled vehicle, and in 1884 the first automobile or car (shortened from "motor carriage," no doubt) was built. A motor car needs no horse to pull it. It is entirely enclosed and has comfortable seats. The driver sits in the front seat and guides the vehicle with a steering wheel. Curiously, the power that moves it forward is measured in "horse power"!

A few days ago, on a return visit to the UK, I witnessed a carriage with four horses driving through the Hampshire countryside. It was a powerful sight and I can understand why you were often frightened. It is not difficult to imagine how the passengers in the carriage were tossed from side to side!

I have actually witnessed carriage rides—yes, this has been made possible through the magic of cinematography, or "moving pictures"—movies, we call them, or films.

At the Château Tocqueville, it is as if the portraits mounted on the walls were able to talk and move. I mention this because a film I was watching recently told the story of another now famous Hampshire lady. Her name was Jane Austen. Jane was born in Steventon, Hampshire in 1775 and she died in Winchester in 1817, when you were eighteen. Possibly you were living in Paris at the time, with your aunt and uncle, Elizabeth and Thomas Belam. History tells us that in Jane's time it was not thought "proper" for women to be authors, or for their works to be published. Succeeding generations have benefited greatly from the characters Jane Austen created and from her insight into the life and times of the 18th and 19th centuries. I am one of those persons.

Alas, I have wandered away from the *Tocqueville* ferry!

My search for you and your story has consumed my life. I have discovered that in each letter I will need to find parallels between your life and mine. I am convinced that human nature really doesn't change. We adapt to the times and centuries we are born into.

I enjoy your company, as I'm sure I would have, if we had met at the Château those many years ago. Eagerly I look forward to further correspondence with you.

With fond regards,
Sheila Le Sueur

7

Mary, Alexis & Democracy in America

The château was a welcome retreat for Alexis's colleagues and close friends, one of whom, Gustave de Beaumont, Mary first met in Versailles at the time she first met Alexis. Both Alexis and Gustave shared the same aristocratic backgrounds, had similar temperaments and the same thirst for exploring the ideas of the philosophers and social commentators of The Enlightenment. Their life histories are virtual mirror images. In their voyages together to America, England and Algeria, they co-authored books, and in France they entered the legislature together.

At that time any type of travel was difficult. Trips across the ocean were major voyages. Today's seven-hour or less plane flights across the ocean translated during the nineteenth century into several weeks at sea. For Mary and Alexis this meant long months of separation. This was even before telephones—did the world actually exist before that time?!! It was not until 1876 that the first patent for a telephone was issued. Hand-written letters delivered by stagecoach across land and steamship across oceans was the only means of communication besides actual physical visits.

Apparently Alexis found it extremely difficult to be separated from Mary. Among Beaumont's published works that included the editing of Alexis's autobiography, is Beaumont's observation about his friend:

> When one considers that on the rare occasions when he was separated from her, he never passed a single day without

> writing and giving her a full account of all that he did and felt, the value of such letters and the light that they would throw upon the heart and character of the writer, can easily be imagined.[83]

Alexis's Political Paradox

In 1835, when Alexis and Mary were married, the Royalists were once more in power; the Bourbon dynasty had been restored. Alexis's father was a loyal royalist prefect and in 1827, he had been made a peer of France by Charles X. Privilege and entitlement—a man "more equal than most" was exactly the issue that his youngest son Alexis was grappling with. All his life, Alexis had depended on status as an aristocrat. If not for his father's influence, would Alexis have been able to obtain his position as assistant magistrate in Versailles? And then one may

---

[83] *Alexis de Tocqueville, Memoir, Letters, and Remains of Alexis de Tocqueville, vol. 1* [1861]; Vol. 1 of a 2 volume collection of material originally edited by Gustave de Beaumont after his death. Vol. 1 contains an autobiography, some previously unpublished essays, France before the Consulate, and letters; The text is in the public domain. http://oll.libertyfund.org/titles/2435

ask, if Alexis had not been stationed in Versailles, would he have met Mary Mottley?

Life is filled with ironies. Alexis had little sympathy for his father's and other royalists' political views. One would imagine that conversation between the two was somewhat stilted or they may have avoided political discussions altogether.

Alexis had already been strongly influenced by the lectures of historian and statesman Francois Guizot (1787-1874), who firmly believed that the aristocracy and a privileged caste or class system would soon be a phenomenon of the past. Like other Liberals, Alexis had steeped himself in English history as a model of political development. He had already established strong relationships with Henry Reeve and John Stuart Mills, two British liberal thinkers and writers.

Since Alexis had chosen politics as his vocation and he was a liberal thinker, perhaps it was fitting that he should marry a commoner and break with his family tradition. One could say that Alexis's marriage to Mary Mottley was a personal declaration of his independence.

Democracy in America

In *Democracy in America*, a compilation of observations gathered from interviews, readings and discussions with several Americans well-schooled on the subject of democracy, Alexis was impressed by much of what he saw in America. Relentlessly he pursued his search for a clear understanding of equality. For it was equality—equal status, equal rights, equal living conditions, that was the backbone of democracy. Would the young country of America be successful if it continued to implement a feudal system of plantations or "fiefdoms" that depended on slave labor to work the land? What about the subjugation of Native Americans—and women?

In 1848 the first women's rights convention in the world, organized by Lucretia Mott and Elizabeth Cady Stanton, active members of the abolitionist movement, was held in Seneca Falls, New York. In 1863, shortly after the appearance of *Democracy in America* in France, Stanton and Susan B. Anthony formed the Woman's National Loyal League to support the Thirteenth Amendment to abolish slavery and to campaign for full citizenship for blacks and women.[84]

Alexis must have seen the flaws here in the New World, yet at the same time he was an optimist. The United States Constitution coupled with the Declaration of Independence, had taken a strong stand on equality. Reforms didn't happen overnight. He realized that America, like France, was in the midst of growing pains. Alexis firmly believed that a properly organized society

[84] http://www.historynet.com/womens-suffrage-movement

would provide the necessary foundation for preserving the basic human rights of equality, liberty and fraternity.[85]

Alexis also recognized some of the pitfalls of democracy. When leveling the playing field, it was important to retain individuality. Equal did not mean "uniform." Assimilation did not mean surrender of one's uniqueness. He felt that a society of individuals lacked the intermediate social structures, such as those provided by traditional hierarchies, to mediate relations with the state. The result could end up being a democratic "tyranny of the majority" in which individual rights were compromised.

Tocqueville's works shaped 19th-century discussions of liberalism and equality, and were rediscovered in the 20th century as sociologists debated the causes and cures of tyranny. *Democracy in America* remains widely read and even more

[85] Ibid.

widely quoted by politicians, philosophers, historians and anyone seeking to understand the American character.

Writes Hon. John T. Morgan in the Special Introduction to *Democracy in America:*

> ...When, in 1831, Alexis de Tocqueville came to study Democracy in America, the trial of nearly a half-century of the working of our system had been made, and it had been proved, by many crucial tests, to be a government of "liberty regulated by law," with such results in the development of strength, in population, wealth, and military and commercial power, as no age had ever witnessed.
>
> De Tocqueville had a special inquiry to prosecute, in his visit to America, in which his generous and faithful soul and the powers of his great intellect were engaged in the patriotic effort to secure to the people of France the blessings that Democracy

in America had ordained and established throughout nearly the entire Western Hemisphere. He had read the story of the French Revolution, much of which had been recently written in the blood of men and women of great distinction who were his progenitors; and had witnessed the agitations and terrors of the Restoration and of the Second Republic, fruitful in crime and sacrifice, and barren of any good to mankind.

He had just witnessed the spread of republican government through all the vast continental possessions of Spain in America, and the loss of her great colonies. He had seen that these revolutions were accomplished almost without the shedding of blood, **and he was filled with anxiety to learn the causes that had placed republican government, in France, in such contrast with Democracy in America. [Boldface mine]**

De Tocqueville was scarcely thirty years old when he began his studies of Democracy in America. It was a bold effort for one who had no special training in government, or in the study of political economy, but he had the example of Lafayette in establishing the military foundation of these liberties, and of Washington, Jefferson, Madison, and Hamilton, all of whom were young men, in building upon the Independence of the United States that wisest and best plan of general government that was ever devised for a free people.

He found that the American people, through their chosen representatives who were instructed by their wisdom and experience and were supported by their virtues—cultivated, purified and ennobled by self-reliance and the love of God—had matured, in the excellent wisdom of their counsels, a new plan of government, which embraced every security for their liberties and equal rights and privileges to all in the pursuit of happiness. **He came as an honest and impartial student**

and his great commentary, like those of Paul, was written for the benefit of all nations and people and in vindication of truths that will stand for their deliverance from monarchical rule, while time shall last. [Boldface mine]

A French aristocrat of the purest strain of blood and of the most honorable lineage, whose family influence was coveted by crowned heads; who had no quarrel with the rulers of the nation, and was secure against want by his inherited estates; **was moved by the agitations that compelled France to attempt to grasp suddenly the liberties and happiness we had gained in our revolution and, by his devout love of France, to search out and subject to the test of reason the basic principles of free government that had been embodied in our Constitution. This was the mission of De Tocqueville, and no mission was ever more honorably or justly conducted, or concluded with greater éclat, or better results for the welfare of mankind. [Boldface mine]**

His researches were logical and exhaustive. They included every phase of every question that then seemed to be apposite to the great inquiry he was making.

The judgment of all who have studied his commentaries seems to have been unanimous, that his talents and learning were fully equal to his task. He began with the physical geography of this country, and examined the characteristics of the people, of all races and conditions, their social and religious sentiments, their education and tastes; their industries, their commerce, their local governments, their passions and prejudices, and their ethics and literature; leaving nothing unnoticed that might afford an argument to prove that our plan and form of government was or was not adapted especially to a peculiar people, or that it would be impracticable in any different country, or among any different people.

The pride and comfort that the American people enjoy in the great commentaries of De Tocqueville are far removed from the selfish adulation that comes from a great and singular success. **It is the consciousness of victory over a false theory of government which has afflicted mankind for many ages, that gives joy to the true American, as it did to De Tocqueville in his great triumph. [Boldface mine]**

We are frequently indebted to him for able expositions and true doctrines relating to subjects that have slumbered in the minds of the people until they were suddenly forced on our attention by unexpected events.

If M. De Tocqueville could now search for a law that would negative [sic.] this provision in its effect upon social equality, he would fail to find it. But he would find it in the unwritten law of the natural aversion of the races. **He would find it in public opinion, which is the vital force in every law in a**

free government. This is a subject that our Constitution failed to regulate, because it was not contemplated by its authors. It is a question that will settle itself, without serious difficulty. [boldface mine]

The test of moral character and devotion to the duties of good citizenship are ignored in the laws, because the courts can seldom deal with such questions in a uniform and satisfactory way, under rules that apply alike to all. Thus the voter, selected by law to represent himself and four other non-voting citizens, is often a person who is unfit for any public duty or trust. In a town government, having a small area of jurisdiction, where the voice of the majority of qualified voters is conclusive, the fitness of the person who is to exercise that high representative privilege can be determined by his neighbors and acquaintances, and, in the great majority of cases, it will be decided honestly and for the good of the country. In such meetings, there is always a spirit of loyalty to the State, because that is loyalty to the people, and a reverence for God that gives weight to the duties and responsibilities of citizenship.

M. De Tocqueville found in these minor local jurisdictions the theoretical conservatism which, in the aggregate, is the safest reliance of the State. So we have found them, in practice, the true protectors of the purity of the ballot, without which all free government will degenerate into absolutism.

In the future of the Republic, we must encounter many difficult and dangerous situations, but the principles established in the Constitution and the check upon hasty or inconsiderate legislation, and upon executive action, and the supreme arbitrament of the courts, will be found sufficient for the safety of personal rights, and for the safety of the government, and the prophetic outlook of M. De Tocqueville will be fully realized through the influence of Democracy in America. **Each succeeding generation of Americans will find in**

> **the pure and impartial reflections of De Tocqueville a new source of pride in our institutions of government, and sound reasons for patriotic effort to preserve them and to inculcate their teachings. They have mastered the power of monarchical rule in the American Hemisphere, freeing religion from all shackles, and will spread, by a quiet but resistless influence, through the islands of the seas to other lands, where the appeals of De Tocqueville for human rights and liberties have already inspired the souls of the people. [boldface mine]**[86]

The publishing of *Democracy in America* won Alexis the title of political scientist. He was named to the Legion of Honour, the Academy of Moral and Political Sciences (1838), and the French Academy (1841). Soon the book was published in England, Belgium, Germany, Spain, Hungary, Denmark, and Sweden. In the United States it became a classic and to this day it has retained that status. In the college classroom it is part of the standard

[86] https://www.gutenberg.org/files/815/815-h/815-h.htm#link2H_INTR

reading list for introductory courses in American History and Political Sciences.

The final portion of *Democracy in America* was published in 1840. In these sections of the work, Alexis broadened his thesis to consider the influence of equality on all aspects of modern society. Using France as his main example, he observed that since 1830 when the Liberals came into power, the government had been slowly curtailing many liberties. He also observed growing state intervention. His chapters on democratic individualism and centralization in *Democracy in America* contained a new warning based on these observations. He argued that a mild, stagnant despotism was the greatest threat to democracy.[87]

In 1839, as the second volume of *Democracy in America* neared publication, Tocqueville reentered political life, serving as a deputy in the French assembly. By this time in his political career, Alexis was so deeply ensconced in politics, speechmaking

87 Ibid.

and writing, he was happy to give Mary full responsibility of all domestic matters at the Château. Mary proved to be an excellent manager and bookkeeper. When required, she did not hesitate to make decisions and apparently was competent when meeting other domestic challenges as well. A frugal person, she was never without a private income of her own.

Alexis was well aware of the lack of strong leadership at a time when it was critically necessary. He had already prophesied revolution a few weeks before it occurred.

From Paris in May, 1848, Alexis wrote the following to his cousin, the Countess Louis de Kergorlay:

> If the newspapers you read, dear cousin, tell you that we are going from bad to worse, that the confidence of the people in their rulers is nearly gone, that our financial difficulties are

increasing, that want and misery become more prevalent, and that every day everything falls into a state of greater confusion, they must give you a correct notion of our condition. Such is, indeed the present aspect of affairs, and if some great man does not fall from the clouds within the next few months to extricate us, I greatly fear that we shall not escape without going through the bitter experience of anarchy, civil war, and their ruinous consequences. Now as I see no signs of this great man, and, in fact, have no faith in the sudden apparition of heroes, while I see around me swarms of mischievous pigmies, I am very uneasy and much alarmed. If so many of my friends and relations were not exposed to the storm, the eager interest awakened in me by the singular, at times imposing scene before me, might, perhaps reconcile me to it. I was so wearied by the monotony of the previous period, that I have no right to complain of the stormy variety of this world as the passing scenes in a play, and to me they are far more.[88]

---

[88] Op. Cit., Tocqueville, Alexis de. *Memoir, Letters & Remembrances.* Vol. II, p. 98.

This letter was written at a time when Alexis's frustration over the turmoil in the streets and in the halls of government was fueled by his own inner conflict. Alexis was a politician for all times, but the "times" did not always understand him. Is this not a universal dilemma that almost every notable individual has faced throughout history?

During the Revolution of 1848, the paradoxes that plagued Alexis in his own aristocratic background became even more evident when France was faced with a politically awakened working class. The country was ripe for a socialist revolution. Tocqueville considered economic independence necessary to the preservation of his own intellectual independence. How then could he reconcile his beliefs with the reality of the poor, clamoring for a welfare state?

For Alexis, economic dependency was not a virtue, but how could equality be established when the poor were unemployed and when dependency opened the floodgates for "universal and degrading dependence on the state by all social classes"?[89]

"Unsympathetic to revolutionaries and contemptuous of socialists before the revolution, Tocqueville opposed the demands of the Parisian workers during the June days of 1848, when their uprising was bloodily suppressed by the military dictator General Louis Cavaignac, as well as in the debates over the constitution of 1848. The only intellectual change produced in Tocqueville by the events of 1848 was a recognition of the strength of socialist ideas and of the problematic nature of the proprietary society. **Although he had sought to reconcile the aristocracy to liberal democracy in Democracy in America, he rejected social democracy as it emerged in 1848 as incompatible with liberal democracy."[Boldface mine.]**[90]

---

[89] http://www.britannica.com/biography/Alexis-de-Tocqueville

[90] Ibid.

After the Revolution, Alexis was elected as a conservative Republican to the Constituent Assembly and he was nominated to the committee that wrote the constitution of the Second Republic. In the following year he became vice president of the Assembly.

President Louis-Napoléon Bonaparte dismissed Alexis in October 1849, following which Alexis suffered a physical collapse. Upon recovery he attempted to avert the final confrontation between the president and the legislature. This ended in an executive seizure of dictatorial power. Alexis was briefly imprisoned for opposing Louis-Napoléon's coup d'état on December 2, 1851 and he was deprived of all political offices for refusing his oath of loyalty to the new regime.

For Alexis, public life was over. He retired to his family estate in Normandy and began writing a history of modern France, the first volume of which was published as *The Old Regime and the*

French Revolution (1856). Alexis blamed the French Revolution on corruption among the nobility and on the political disillusionment of the French population. Briefly, he pointed out that France seemed less the democratic society of the future he had glimpsed in America than the prisoner of its own past.[91] Ironically, *The Old Regime* reaffirmed the libertarian example of the Anglo-American world.

"The acclaim that greeted this study briefly dispelled the gloom of his last years... The nine-volume publication of his works, edited by Beaumont (1860–66), was received as the legacy of a martyr of liberty. In England his name was invoked during the franchise reform debates of the 1860s, and in Germany it was linked to controversies over liberalization and federalization in the years preceding the empire devised by Otto von Bismarck.

---

[91] Ibid.

"...Nevertheless, the classless society had failed to appear in Europe, and America seemed to have become European by becoming nationalist and imperialist."[92]

Once again a public figure, he made a visit to England in 1857 that culminated in an audience with the prince consort and was the last public triumph of his life. He returned to his work, but, before he could finish his study of the Revolution, he was already struggling with tuberculosis. In 1959, he collapsed and died, with his family at his bedside."[93]

Perhaps Alexis can be categorized among many great men and women whose accomplishments were not wholly appreciated during their lifetime. The impact of his works in the 20th and 21st centuries surely would have astonished him.

---

92 Ibid.

93 Ibid.

"It seems certain that Tocqueville will continue to be invoked as an authority and inspiration by those sharing his contempt of static authoritarian societies as well as his belief in the final disappearance of class divisions and in liberty as the ultimate political value."[94]

[94] Ibid.

8

Life in 19th Century England & France

Health Care

People in 19th century England, France and America suffered from many of the same illnesses as we do today. The difference was the fact that the treatments at that time were ineffective and often more painful than their original complaints.

At the beginning of the 19th century, all diseases were believed to be the result of fluid excess. The prescribed cures were purging, vomiting, bleeding and blistering, procedures which were believed to restore the patient's natural balance of the body systems, known as the "four humors" (blood, phlegm, and black and yellow bile).

Surgery was always a last resort, as it was extremely painful and often deadly. The only available early anesthetics were opium and alcohol. By the 1840s drugs such as chloroform, nitrous oxide, and ether began to be used by high society as social drugs, and were eventually used in surgery. With the introduction of anesthetics, the often extremely intense pain of surgery was removed. This pain-free state allowed for longer and more complex operations.

Physical examinations were limited to assessing the pulse and respiratory rates and appearance of the urine.

At that time theoretical medicine was considered "scientific" and practical medicine was referred to as "alternative." Homeopathy was highly regarded and practiced by many. Other practices included Thomsonianism, phrenology (skull morphology), mesmerism, electropathy and hydropathy. The art of healing was relatively unknown to Europeans and Americans, unless their travels had taken them to India and the Orient, where they may have learned of the practices of acupuncture, herbology, Ayurvedic medicine, and other highly advanced practices. Probably they would have scoffed at these procedures, considering them quackery similar to the snake oil liniments and salves peddled by charlatans in America and abroad.

Mary suffered from lumbago and kidney problems. Later in life she developed rheumatism. At that time there were no mild analgesics and certainly no over the counter medications available to ease her pain. It is doubtful that she resorted to narcotics such as opium, morphine or alcohol. Aspirin was not discovered yet, and then only by accident in 1897 when a chemist named Felix Hoffman was searching for something to relieve his father's rheumatism. By synthesizing a stable form of salicylic acid powder, which is merely an imitation of willow root, a naturally grown herb, Hoffman stumbled across one of today's best known analgesics.

During the 19th century many other chemists were also using herbs in order to develop the first pharmaceuticals. It was reported that 121 prescription medications were derived from plants, and close to 74% were discovered because of their use in herbal healing.[95]

In the US, physicians changed the focus from total body healing or going to the source of the issue, to diagnosing and treating the presenting symptoms. Three US doctors encouraged this shift in medical thought. The first doctor, Dr. Daniel Drake, attempted to standardize medical practice in 1819 when he founded the Medical College of Ohio in Cincinnati. The second doctor, a US Army doctor, Dr. William Beaumont, took advantage of a tragic situation to study the structure and function of the digestive

---

95 http://www.longwoodherbal.org/herbs/02_history.htm

system: he studied the stomach wound of a military patient. This wound wouldn't heal, so Beaumont studied the workings of the stomach through this lesion. In 1833 he was able to publish a work on the chemistry of digestion titled "Experiments and Observations on the Gastric Juice and Physiology of Digestion."

The third doctor, Dr. Samuel Gross, author of *A System of Surgery; Pathological, Diagnostic, Therapeutic, and Operative.* lectured at the Jefferson Medical College in Philadelphia on improved surgical techniques.[96]

In 1816, Rene-Theophile Hyacinthe Laënnec (1781-1826), a brilliant French physician, invented the stethoscope. Known as the father of pulmonary medicine, Laënnec 's stethoscope accurately described the physical signs of pulmonary disease, including pulmonary consumption, bronchiectasis, pneumothorax, cancer of the lung, empyema, and pneumonia.

96 http://www.onlinehealthcaredegrees.com/resources/health-history-19th-century-medicine/

Legend has it that the idea of inventing a stethoscope came to him when he watched children talking to one another through a hollow log while playing on the grounds of the Louvre.

It was not until X-rays were discovered in 1895 by a German scientist, Wilhelm Rontgen, that the anatomical structures could be confirmed on film. Sadly, this breakthrough in medicine came too late for Dr. Laennec to view by X-ray the anatomical structures he so aptly described.

Dr. Laënnec, known as one of the greatest clinicians of all time, died in 1826 from Tuberculosis, a disease he first described and spent his life trying to eradicate—and the disease that ultimately claimed Alexis de Tocqueville's life.

Antoine Redier, a French historian, describes Mary as having yellow teeth.[97] Although this may be true, she surely wasn't the only individual at that time with this problem. The causes are easily identified. If one drank water from a well that was contaminated with minerals or if they experienced childhood fevers, the teeth could yellow.

In 1859 when Alexis became seriously ill, apparently Mary's eyesight was poor and her overall health was also declining. She died in 1864, surviving Alexis by only five years, and was buried beside him in the churchyard in the small village of Tocqueville, where her birth date inscribed on the tomb is incorrect.

Alexis was 54 when he died, and Mary was 63. Based on today's standards, both would have been considered relatively young, Alexis scarcely past middle age and Mary just entering a time of life when she might begin to experience physical challenges.

---

97 http://oll.libertyfund.org/pages/alexis-de-tocqueville-a-bibliographical-essay-by-john-lukacs

One may wish to point out at that the average life expectancy in the 19th century was only 45-50 years old. However, this is based on mathematical fallacies that include in this "average" statistic the high infant mortality rate at that time. In general, people in the 18th and 19th centuries lived nearly as long as we do today.[98]

Treatment for Tuberculosis in the 19th Century

Alexis was considered to be a delicate child who suffered from frequent colds and chest infections. In his late forties and fifties, he developed pulmonary tuberculosis. No effective therapies existed at that time for TB.

The prescribed treatments were excruciating. One treatment, known as "cupping" or "blistering" was thought to act as a

---

98 If one would take the time to read journals of the period, or census records of long ago they would find a good majority of adults living to a ripe old age. Just for our own information, let's look at the age of death from some of our Founding generation: Thomas Jefferson was 83 when he died, John Adams was 90, George Washington was a young 67 - but he died due to blood loss from the then popular medical procedure bloodletting, George Wythe was 80, Paul Revere was 83, and Ben Franklin was 84. As you can see, even in America's colonial period it wasn't unusual to see people living to a ripe old age. http://passionforthepast.blogspot.com/2011/08/average-life-expectancy-myth.html

counter irritant. It involved applying glass cups that were heated and applied to superficial incisions in the skin. As they cooled a vacuum was created, thus producing blisters on the skin. This, it was believed, released the "vapors."

Alexis also was treated with "blood letting" by applying leeches to his chest wall or venesection. This was a procedure that involved making an incision in a vein and draining the blood. Purgatives and emetics were popular and freely administered. Alexis's condition was only exacerbated by such radical treatments, leaving him exhausted.

It was thought that sunshine and warm climates were therapeutic. Those who were able to afford this therapy followed the doctors' advice. Mary and Alexis traveled to the south of France to escape from the damp winters in Normandy.

In *The Making of a Social Disease: Tuberculosis in 19th Century France,* David S. Barnes traces the evolution of tuberculosis in 19th century France from a romantic disease of "heightened sensibility" to its reconstruction as a social disease and a social problem. Consumption, as it was known, was the fatal disease of the femme fatale portrayed in countless works of fiction that appeared during this time.

Nineteenth century Paris and other urban centers of France, particularly its port cities, were imploding. In less than 30 years during the first half of the 19th century, Paris's population doubled. Thousands of mostly poor migrants from the countryside and provincial cities flooded the city. Poor sewage, absence of any type of rubbish disposal system causing filth everywhere, factory stench and poor personal hygiene were open invitations for contagious diseases. One can imagine what it must have been like living in a cesspool. Nineteenth and 20th

century British, French, German and Russian writers delivered vivid descriptions of these deplorable conditions.

Curiously, states Barnes, "in France, as far as the etiology [cause] of disease is concerned, a better term might be 'essentialist medicine': the belief that disease in general (and tuberculosis in particular) was part of a person's *essence.* Illness, in this view, arose spontaneously from internal causes and constitutional predisposition rather than from external causes, although external factors could influence the outcome of internal tendencies and predispositions."[99]

Some doctors believed that certain individuals had a genetic disposition for acquiring TB. They referred to this as an "epidemic constitution." This inherited tendency was passed on from one generation to the next.

---

[99] http://publishing.cdlib.org/ucpressebooks/view?docId=ft8t1nb5rp&chunk.id=s1.1.1&toc.depth=1&toc.id=ch1&brand=ucpress

Laënnec was a strong proponent of the contagion theory (exposure through individuals with TB, poor hygiene, poor sanitation, etc.). He stated in his widely accepted treatise, *Traité de l'auscultation médiate*: "children of consumptives are more frequently attacked by this disease than are other subjects."[100]

According to Barnes:

> The two chief factors invoked by the hereditarians were sorrowful passions and unhealthy sexual activity (including masturbation and "venereal excesses"). Both of these factors reinforced the impression that disorders such as tuberculosis were part of an individual's essence. Neither factor was innate, certainly, but both were widely portrayed (in romantic and postromantic literature, among other genres) as aspects of fate, intimately related to identity and individuality.

---

[100] Ibid.

> *Implicit* was the conclusion that medicine was therapeutically impotent in the matter (no consolation, not even time itself, could heal these emotional wounds). The passage also came closer than most such texts to explaining the epidemiology of tuberculosis, or at least its concentration in large cities.[101]

Those who died of a broken heart were likely to have suffered from consumption (TB). The broken heart syndrome was not hereditary, however. This type of doubletalk served to explain the inexplicable at a time when testing protocols were relatively non-existent. What you couldn't explain, you blamed on whatever explanation seemed possible, or likely.

The romantic notion of consumption or TB caused by a broken heart or some other type of despair may not have been so absurd after all. Today, with the emergence of mind-body medicine we find that "the concept that the mind is important in health and

---

[101] Ibid.

illness dates back to ancient times."[102] Only in the West during the Renaissance and Enlightenment, or the time in which Mary Mottley and Alexis de Tocqueville lived, was it believed that the mind and body were separate.

According to the National Institute of Health:

> Increasing numbers of scientific and technological discoveries furthered this split and led to an emphasis on disease-based models, pathological changes, and external cures. The role of mind and belief in health and illness began to re-enter Western health care in the 20th century, led by discoveries about pain control via the placebo effect and effects of stress on health. Mind-body medicine focuses on the interactions among the brain, the rest of the body, the mind, and behavior.
>
> The ways in which emotional, mental, social, spiritual, experiential, and behavioral factors can directly affect health.

[102] http://report.nih.gov/nihfactsheets/viewfactsheet.aspx?csid=102

> The National Center for Complementary and Alternative Medicine (NCCAM) is the component of the NIH that studies complementary and alternative medicine (CAM). Within CAM, some examples of mind-body medicine practices are meditation, hypnosis, tai chi, and yoga. [103]

It was not until the 20th century that the cause for Tuberculosis was finally isolated. From then on, patients were treated in sanatoriums where they were placed on bed rest, served a balanced diet, and confined to wards that were built facing the sun. The beds were pushed outside for the benefit of sunshine and fresh air whenever possible.

Sanitation Improvements – Greatest Medical Advancement in the 19th Century

In 1847, Hungarian physician Ignaz Semmelweis (1818–1865) introduced the notion that physicians needed to wash their hands before assisting women with their childbirths. It sounds foolish and archaic to the modern mind to consider that people

[103] Ibid.

could even doubt the importance of cleanliness as a prophylactic against disease. Yet it was not until almost 20 years later when, in 1865 Joseph Lister, a British surgeon, proved the principles of antisepsis with regards to wound treatments that the medical community as well as lay persons began to consider the idea of sanitation as a contributing factor to disease.[104]

By the 1880s, several years after the deaths of both Mary and Alexis, US surgeon Dr. William Mayo began practicing antiseptic surgery. Other contributing factors for addressing infectious diseases were improvements in public health and nutrition as well as sanitation.[105]

Cocaine and Opium

Cocaine was legal even as late as 1885, and was not considered harmful in moderate doses. Many other drugs, now restricted by

---

104 http://www.planetseed.com/relatedarticle/rise-scientific-medicinethe-nineteenth-century

105 Ibid.

law, were also legal then, including opium, which was sold under city permit on the streets of Victoria.

In the nineteenth century many substances, such as mercury and lead, were used as medicines and are now known to be harmful over the long term. "Patent medicines," like Cocaine Toothache Drops, were very popular and required no prescription; they were indeed "For sale by all druggists."[106]

Cholera, Influenza, Typhus, Smallpox, Dysentary

Fifty-two thousand people died from the Asiatic cholera outbreak of 1831. Originating in Bengal, it took five years to arrive in England. Even though the disease could be identified, at first doctors had no clues regarding its cause, treatment or prevention. Later they learned it was caused by contaminated water.

---

[106] Ibid.

Influenza in the form of eight different epidemics over a period of 16 years beginning in 1833, also claimed the lives of thousands. Typhoid and smallpox epidemics raging at the same time as Cholera and Influenza, also claimed tens of thousands of lives.

In his "Report on the Sanitary Condition of the Labouring Population of Gt. Britain," Edwin Chadwick included figures to show that in 1839 for every person who died of old age or violence, eight died of specific diseases. This helps explain why during the second and third decades of the nineteenth century nearly one infant in three in England failed to reach the age of five.[107]

Hospital Care

Nineteenth century hospitals were more like prisons. Often as many as 50-100 patients were crowded into wards that were small, dark, bleak, and littered with filth. There was no understanding of nutrition; the food they received was totally

[107] Ibid.

inadequate for their needs. Sanitary conditions were poor or non-existent and disease was rampant. The death rate was appalling. Even the basics, such as soap and water, went unrecognized and surgical instruments were passed from one patient to another.

It is not surprising that when people became ill they preferred to remain in their homes rather than check into a hospital. Hospitals were viewed as places to die, and it is difficult to disagree with that opinion. Nevertheless, even though no one can deny that modern medical technologies and hospital care are vastly improved since then, the death rate caused by today's hospital care is still alarmingly high.[108]

---

[108] Hospital Errors are the Third Leading Cause of Death in U.S., and New Hospital Safety Scores Show Improvements Are Too Slow...Washington, D.C., October 23, 2013 – New research estimates up to 440,000 Americans are dying annually from preventable hospital errors. **This puts medical errors as the third leading cause of death in the United States, underscoring the need for patients to protect themselves and their families from harm, and for hospitals to make patient safety a priority.**
http://www.hospitalsafetyscore.org/newsroom/display/hospitalerrors-thirdleading-causeofdeathinus-improvementstooslow

In the 19th century, medical care was both feared and distrusted; in fairness to the physicians, their medical education was neither formalized nor regulated. As medical schools evolved, a class structure developed within them. Those educated in the universities were considered to be the most knowledgeable and their primary responsibility was to examine, diagnose and prescribe medicines. However, they were not allowed to perform surgery.

Surgery

In the 19th century, surgeons were regarded as craftsman who received their education by being apprenticed to an apothecary. They performed operations often without the benefit of anesthesia, reduced fractures, and treated accidents and skin diseases. Surgeons were considered to be less skilled than physicians because they worked "outside" of the body.

Apothecaries were powerful groups of men who were educated by being apprenticed to a skilled tradesman for five years. They compounded medicines, sold them and provided medical advice. Surgeons' salaries were much lower on the pay scale compared to those of the university-trained physicians. Usually they found it necessary to augment their salaries and skills by becoming apothecaries. This allowed them to dispense and sell the medications.

Nursing

In the Middle Ages, care of the ailing, the destitute and lepers was delegated to Catholic orders. For the most part these caregivers had nothing to offer except comfort and compassion. During the Reformation, these religious houses were either razed to the ground or converted into government buildings.

Caring for the sick was considered women's work, but now that the Catholic orders had been abolished, it was difficult to find caregivers. People usually recruited elderly women to serve as nurses. Sobriety among these women was a continual problem. It was thought to be a great help if the women could write or at least sign their name.

In the early 19th century the religious orders returned and once more women played an important role. Their responsibilities were two-fold: education of the youth and care of the sick. In Paris at that time a group of women came together and formed the order of Bon Secours. They introduced the radical idea of caring for the sick in their own homes, both during the day and at night. According to church rule, sisters were normally behind their convent walls by nightfall, but the order of Bon Secours was able to obtain permission to practice their theory for a year. At the end of the probationary period they had proved that this innovative care of the sick was successful; consequently, the sisters won the respect of the laity and the church.

The Bishop recognized the work of the sisters by naming himself as founder of the order and provided the statutes that were to rule the new congregation. Thus the congregation of the Sisters of Bon Secours was formed. Their mission was, as it remains today, humility, poverty, and charity. During periods of unrest and revolutions the Sisters continued to faithfully fulfill their mission to care for the poor and the unwanted.

Conditions in England were much the same. Most recognized the need for nurses to care for the sick, but the concept of nursing as an honorable profession never materialized until the middle of the century. At that time, Florence Nightingale left behind her privileged status and dedicated her life to cleaning up the hospitals and established a nursing school at St. Thomas hospital in London.

The nucleus of Nightingale's nursing staff came from young women from privileged families where the eldest daughters were required to make a good marriage. The younger women from these families embraced the nursing profession as a refuge from serving as a companion or a governess. Nurses had an opportunity for education while simultaneously caring for those less fortunate than themselves. Their chosen path was not an easy one. It involved hard work with long hours and poor pay. St. Thomas Hospital's nursing program established the foundation for today's nursing profession.

Communications

It is difficult to imagine a time without radios, movies, television, the Internet, videos, DVDs, social media, 24/7 news on iPads, tablets, laptops, desk computers, smartphones, AM/FM radio, and short wave. It is also hard to believe that printed newspapers, the only existing media other than books and pamphlets during Mary Mottley's time, are being replaced by Internet news companies and eZines. In one of the sample news items printed in this book, you may have noticed that it took three days for the

Portsmouth Tribune to receive a report of war news from Paris. Livestream Internet media technologies have transformed the journalism world.

The Postal Service

Postal systems existed as early as 1000 BC when the Egyptian government dispatches were delivered by horse or horse-drawn wagon. In the 6th century the Persians used a relay system of riders who stopped at regularly placed post houses to deposit their official documents. They then proceeded on a fresh horse, or another messenger completed the journey, tandem style.

In 1122-221 BC, the Chinese conveyed their official documents by couriers. The Romans, whose territory spread throughout the entire Mediterranean area, created the most reliable system, similar to one that was used by the Chinese. They named the system *cursus publicus*, a public course that was a series of state-sponsored roads with relay stations. In a 24-hour period the messengers, depending on the weather and the route conditions, were able to travel approximately 170 miles.

In the 19th century, writing was an art form and Alexis was surely a master. Friends who received a letter from him knew it was thoughtful, caring and written for them alone.

"To Tocqueville, letter writing was a need; it widened the circle of his life. He was convinced that friendship is a tender plant that withers without cultivation," wrote Alexis's close friend, Gustave de Beaumont, in a memoir edited after Tocqueville's death.[109]

Letters tended to be long and detailed. They were written with a straight pen that had a split nib and was dipped into India ink. Writing paper was thin; it was expensive and purchased by weight.

In 1831 when Alexis visited America, Mary and Alexis's courtship continued to blossom through the letters they wrote to each

[109] Op. Cit., Tocqueville, Alexis de. *Memoirs, Letters & Remains,* Vol. I, p. 86.

other. Mary loved stories from far away countries. Alexis's tales of American democracy, of the Americans he met during his travels must have delighted her. He had already begun to deeply appreciate the fact that he could share his thoughts and ideas with her.

Letters from America took weeks, sometimes even months before they reached France by steamship. They were delivered in special stagecoaches owned by the post office. Uniform in color, they could be easily recognized. The stagecoaches also offered passenger service, with a space for four passengers inside the coach and eight on the outside.

Mailbags were placed on the top of the coach and luggage was stored in a container below. On each route were specific drop-off points. Passengers whose destinations were not on the regular stagecoach route often found the mail coach to be a more convenient form of transport.

During his political career, Alexis spent several months each year in Paris when the legislature was in session. While he was away, Mary and Alexis communicated daily by post. Their letters to each other usually contained detailed accounts of daily events. Mary's letters would have included management updates for the Château and other social matters.

Postage Stamps

On January 1, 1849 the newly created Second Republic of France became the eighth country in the world to implement adhesive postage stamps for the prepayment of letter mail.[110]

On the *stampcollectingworld.com* website we further learn that:

> In 1849 the new French stamps featured the profile of the Roman goddess Ceres. Ceres was the ancient Roman goddess of agriculture, fertility, and motherly love. It is well known

[110] http://www.stamp-collecting-world.com/frenchstamps.html

that, in ancient Roman life, men ruled the empire, but women were the undisputed masters of the home.

This was a very appropriate symbol for the first French stamps, considering that agriculture is such a huge part of the national economy. In fact, even to modern times, the allegorical representation of the French republic has always been depicted as a heroic female figure.[111]

New French stamps were issued for the 2nd Empire, beginning in 1853. These new stamps, all showing the effigy of Emperor Napoleon III, are very much like the 1849-1850 issues, but the inscription at the top has been changed from "REPUB FRANC" to "EMPIRE FRANC."[112]

Definitive French stamps, featuring a brand new design, were issued between 1876 and 1900.

---

[111] http://www.stamp-collecting-world.com/frenchstamps_1849.html

[112] http://www.stamp-collecting-world.com/frenchstamps_1853.html

> This new design, officially known as the Peace and Commerce Issue, features allegorical images of "Peace" and "Commerce" holding hands above a World globe. In center of the stamp is a white rectangle containing the value. The inscriptions read "POSTE" at the top and "REPUBLIQUE FRANÇAISE" at the bottom.
>
> French stamp collectors, however, prefer to refer to certain stamp issues by the designer's name, rather than the particular motif. In the case of these stamps, the designer was Jules-Auguste Sage, whose name is located in the small imprint at the extreme lower left corner of the design. Thus, philatelists today refer to these as the Type Sage Issues.[113]

In the United States, a 5-cent Benjamin Franklin stamp appeared in 1847.[114] The first stamps appeared in 1847. Some of the most actively collected 19th Century stamps include the Columbian

---

[113] http://www.stamp-collecting-world.com/frenchstamps_1876.html

[114] http://postalmuseum.si.edu/collections/object-spotlight/franklin.html

Commemorative Set printed in 1893, and the famous Western Cattle in a Storm from the Trans-Mississippi set. It also includes the rarest US stamps such as 85A the famous Z grill of which there are only two known.[115]

Transportation

In Alexis's and Mary's time, traveling on land from one place to another meant that one walked or used a coach.[116] The village of Tocqueville was within walking distance from the Château, but when Mary needed to travel farther, a coach was her only option. In 19th century France this was, by necessity, the vehicle of choice, since there was no other means of transportation other than riding horseback. People could travel by boat along the coastline and inland on the canals and other waterways, but if they wanted to travel to places where there were no waterways, they were limited to horses and coaches.

[115] http://brucemacdonaldstamps.com/19th-century-us-stamps-1-293/

[116] http://www.literary-liaisons.com/article033.html

The coaches were manufactured in France, England and Germany. Styles varied from the simple wooden cart used for hauling goods in the country to ultra-elegant stage coaches for royalty in the cities. Some were open and others were covered.

Many attempts were made to improve the comfort and durability of the coach by changing the size of the wheels, strengthening the suspension and making the seats more comfortable.

A staff consisting of a coachman and stable boys cared for the horses. The large elegant carriage houses at the Tocqueville Château are still in existence today.

The trip to Paris, which Alexis made often, took four days, with overnight stops along the way. Since rubber for wheels did not exist yet, depending on the state of the roads the journey must have been far from comfortable. With Mary's health issues that included lumbago and rheumatism, traveling by coach must have been extremely difficult and uncomfortable.

Soon after they were married, Alexis took Mary to Baden-Baden, a spa town in the state of Baden-Württemberg in southwestern Germany, on the banks of the Oos River, close to France and Switzerland. He wrote to his dear friend and cousin, Count Louis de Kergorlay, on October 10, 1836, that Mary (Marie) was suffering from neuralgia. They had spent a month in Berne, Switzerland where the best physicians suggested the waters of Baden would be useful for her condition. However, the treatment was unsuccessful. The journey by coach must have added to her misery.[117]

In 1829, horse drawn omnibuses were introduced in London and by the 1860s, horse drawn trams appeared throughout the country, connecting towns as well as cities. In 1885 and 1886,

---

[117] Op. Cit., Tocqueville, Alexis de. *Memoir, Letters & Remains of Alexis de Tocqueville*, US: BiblioLife, 2009.

Karl Benz and Gottlieb Daimler made the first cars, and the motorbike was patented in 1885. Bicycles also became a popular form of transportation.

By 1815 passenger steamships were crossing the Atlantic Ocean as well as English Channel. Alexis's ocean journey took several weeks. In 1838 the *Sirius* steamship made the journey in 19 days. However, steam did not completely replace sails until the end of the 19th century when the steam turbine was used on ships.

European Waterways – Commercial Transportation

In the 17th century, France took the lead in developing a European canal system, which was expanded during the 18th and 19th centuries:

> In the north the Saint-Quentin Canal, with a 3 1/2-mile tunnel, opened in 1810, linking the North Sea and the Schelde and Lys systems with the English Channel via the Somme and

with Paris and Le Havre via the Oise and Seine. In the interior the Canal du Centre connected the Loire at Digoin with the Sâone at Chalon and completed the first inland route from the English Channel to the Mediterranean; the Sâone and Seine were linked farther north to give a more direct route from Paris to Lyon; the Rhine-Rhône Canal, opened in 1834, provided a direct north-to-south route; while the Sambre-Oise Canal linked the French canal system with the Belgian network via the Meuse. Toward the end of the 19th century, France embarked on the standardization of its canal system to facilitate through communication without transshipment. The ultimate result was a doubling of traffic between the opening of the century and World War II.

Industrial development in the early 19th century prompted Belgium to extend its inland waterways, especially to carry coal from Mons and Charleroi to Paris and northern France. Among the new canals and extensions built were the Mons-

Condé and the Pommeroeul-Antoing canals, which connected the Haine and the Schelde; the Sambre was canalized; the Willebroek Canal was extended southward with the building of the Charleroi-Brussels Canal in 1827; and somewhat later the Campine routes were opened to serve Antwerp and connect the Meuse and Schelde. When the growth of the textile trade in Ghent created a need for better water transport, the Gent Ship Canal, cut through to Terneuzen, was opened in 1827, giving a shorter route to the sea. The Dutch extended their canals to serve the continental European industrial north. The Maastricht-Liège Canal was opened in 1850, enabling raw materials and steel to be transported from the Meuse and Sambre industrial areas by waterway throughout the Netherlands. In 1824 a long ship canal was built to bypass silting that obstructed navigation on the IJsselmeer (Zuiderzee) and to enter the North Sea in the Texel Roads. Later an even shorter ship canal was built to IJmuiden.[118]

---

118 http://www.britannica.com/technology/canal-waterway

Railroads

In 1825, the Stockton and Darlington railway opened in England and by the 1840s most towns were connected by railway. A few months before Alexis's death, he traveled with Mary from Paris to Lyon by rail. Even though the first underground railway in England was built in 1863, it wasn't until 1900 that the Paris Metro opened.[119]

Trains did not reach Normandy until the Paris to Cherbourg line was opened in July of 1858. On this occasion, the Tocquevilles' house guests were Gustave de Beaumont, his wife, Clementine de Lafayette, and a devoted friend, Jean-Charles Rivet, who was the administrator of the Western Railways in France. Mary, Alexis and their guests watched the celebration from the towers of Tourlaville, the Renaissance Château owned by Alexis's brother, Edouard.

---

119 http://www.localhistories.org/transport.html

The four-day celebration was marked by a historic meeting between Queen Victoria and Napoleon III at the port of Cherbourg. The large fleet of 600 English and French ships anchored in the roads off Cherbourg harbor must have been a memorable sight.

The Plight of 19th Century Women

In France only two famous 19th century women are recognized for their accomplishments: Amantine-Lucile-Aurore Dupin, a novelist who wrote under the pseudonym of a male name, "George Sand" in order to get her works published and recognized; and Flora Tristan, an activist from the working classes. Tristan is acknowledged today for the role she played in the women's rights movement, but at the time she would have been marginalized if not ignored.

Among the handful of 19th century British women who achieved recognition are:

- Elizabeth Fry, a Quaker prison reformer
- Queen Victoria, who reigned for more than 60 years
- Florence Nightingale, a reformer of hospitals and the nursing profession
- Dr. James Miranda Barry, a woman who disguised herself as a man in order to practice as a doctor
- Charlotte, Emily, and Anne Bronte, novelists
- Catherine Booth, co-founder of the Salvation Army with her husband, William Booth
- Elizabeth Garrett Anderson, pioneer woman doctor
- Ellen Terry, actress
- Lillie Langtry, actress
- Elizabeth Barrett Browning, poet
- Mary Kingsley, explorer
- Millicent Fawcett, leader of the constitutional suffrage movement[120]

---

[120] https://answers.yahoo.com/question/index?qid=20081101234741AAflmiJ

Young women had little or no choice of a future. To earn a decent living, education or some form of vocational training was a requisite. If this door was closed to them, the only other option was marriage and motherhood. Their verbal nuptial agreement was followed by a wedding ceremony demanding that they obey their husbands and that their bodies by law belonged to their spouses. Sex on demand and motherhood were the order of the day.

If a woman inherited money or land, automatically it became the husband's property. Wealthy widows were exempt, but it is doubtful that they lacked for suitors. Single women who inherited money and who had no desire to marry were financially stable, even though they were treated as social outcasts. It is interesting to suggest that perhaps other women in unhappy marriages envied them.

If life was tough for middle class women, it was even worse for women with little or no means. The class structure in England sentenced them to lives of hard work and drudgery. They were forced to earn their living as domestics, working 12 to 16 hours a day. Usually they lived at their place of employment, slept in a dreary room at the top of several flights of stairs, and worked seven days a week. At least these slave women did not have to go hungry or beg on the streets.

Other women sought factory or farm work as unskilled laborers. Some escaped by emigrating to the colonies. Even though the ratio of men was greater in those countries, women still found themselves in the traditional role of dependency.

In the 1840s one learns of middle-class women who were able to earn money as seamstresses, since this was considered female work. Some chose to set up their business in their homes. Usually they were paid by the piece; wages were low and workdays were long. If they worked away from home, the conditions were dark, damp and extremely unhealthy. Their male employers were often unscrupulous, treating them as chattel and seducing them at will.

Married women without means were forced to work and raise their family as well. Often the only respite for them was the time allotted for recovering from childbirth. If they tried to run away, the police would usually return them to the same miserable situation. Punishment could be severe, since abusive behavior toward women was the norm. They were shamed and made to feel ashamed.

Infidelity was acceptable and generally practiced by men, but if women transgressed, it was not unusual for their children to be taken away from them. Although happy unions must have existed, one would guess they were rare. It is also painful to contemplate the stifled dreams of these women and the music in their souls that was never heard. Just a simple walk in the sunshine or the opportunity to read a good book often was out of their reach.

Poor women in France, especially in the rural areas, were left alone to manage the household and raise the children while their husbands, sons and brothers found work on the "Tour de France," working as migrant workers. There was a practical reason for having large families. The children shouldered responsibility for the family when the father was disabled, ill or too old to work. Sometimes this responsibility fell to the oldest son at an age when he was little more than a child himself.

19th Century Education

As late as the 1870s it was believed that any kind of thought process leading to intellectual stimulation for females would lead to brain fever or barrenness—the greatest sin of all. Women were supposed to be breeders; major emphasis was placed on reproduction.

As mentioned earlier, according to Charles Darwin women lacked intellectual abilities, thus were incapable of being educated. Scientists of the time described women's brains as being smaller than those of men. Nature had delegated women to the "simple task of bearing and nurturing children." Darwin also suggested that If women were not obsessed with their reproductive organs, men certainly were; every malady women suffered from was attributed to the womb.[121] It must have felt like a curse to be a female.

Women of nobility neither worked nor were they formally educated. Often middle class families with a higher income hired a governess to educate their daughters, or they sent them to private academies similar to Mrs. Ewington's academy in Fratton

---

[121] Ibid.

(advertised in the *Portsmouth Telegraph*).[122] The academy focused on feminine virtues, the home and childrearing. Although there is no evidence that Mary attended Mrs. Ewington's Academy, according to the standards of the time, the curriculum would not have included any of the sciences, mathematics or general studies.

Women of the upper middle class were groomed to be mothers, managers of the domestic staff of servants, and decorative companions for husbands upon whom they were completely dependent.

Included in voices of dissent against these barriers to education and other rights for women was Mary Wollstonecraft (1759-1797), author of *Vindication of the Rights of Women*, advocating the equality of the sexes, and a broad curriculum for boys and girls, rich or poor.

---

[122] See *Portsmouth Tribune* sample articles and ads.

Others also criticized the quality of women's private school education. To counter these attacks, parents who sent their daughters to these schools were blamed for insisting that the most important part of any curriculum should focus on instrumental music.

By the end of the 19th century, Florence Nightingale and other feminists pressed for changes in the education of middle-class girls. They stressed the mental equality of women and their ability to sit for the same examinations as male students.

The struggle to obtain equal rights for women in many areas, including education, was long and difficult. Thanks to the efforts of these feminist pioneers, today a woman can receive the same university and postgraduate degrees as a man.

Boys who were born to working class families could spend only a limited time at school. By the age of 11 or 12 they joined the work force. In factories they were subjected to dangerous machinery, forced to climb in and out of chimneys and do other equally treacherous work, often for as long as 12 hours a day. The Industrial Revolution may have brought prosperity, but it also produced a miserable life for the workers, since safe labor laws were still non-existent.

The following is an excerpt of a conversation between Alexis and his friend, Mr. Nasau William Senior, an English economist, recording in Mr. Senior's journal:

> What was the Education, I asked, of women under the *Ancien Regime*?
>
> "The convent," he answered.
>
> "It must have been better," I said, "than the present education, since women of that time were superior to ours."
>
> "It was so far better," he answered, "that it did no harm. A girl at that time was taught nothing. She came from the convent a

> sheet of white paper. Now her mind is a paper scribbled over with trash. The women of that time were thrown into a world far superior to ours, and with sagacity, curiosity, and flexibility of French women, caught knowledge and tact and expression from the men."[123]

Alexis had observed the role of education in a democracy during his 1831 visit to America. In a discussion with his cousin, Louis de Kergolay, he explained:

> Another idea is prevalent in an equal degree; a belief in the wisdom and good sense of mankind; the perfectibility of the human race is contradicted by few, if any. No one denies that the majority may sometimes be mistaken; but they think that in the end it must be right; that is not the sole judge of its own interests, but even the safest, nearest to infallibility. The result

[123] Extract: *Memoirs, Lettres, and Remains of Alexis de Tocquevile, Author of* Democracy in America, translated from the French by the translator of *Napoleon's Correspondence with King Joseph, Vol. 1,* Boston: Ticknor and Fields, 1862. Intra-library loan, courtesy, CUNY Graduate School (New York)

is a belief that education should be bestowed freely on the people, that they can be sufficiently enlightened.

> You remember how often in France we (among) others have puzzled our brains with the question, whether it were to be desired or feared that knowledge should penetrate every class of society. Though so difficult in France, the doubt seems here never to have occurred. I have already propounded the question a hundred times to the most thoughtful men in this country I saw by their summary method of dealing with it that they had never considered it; and that it should even be asked, struck them as shocking and absurd. The diffusion of intelligence, they said, is our only protection against outbreaks of the mob.[124]

In spite of his observations of a democratic society and his profound understanding of the importance of equal

---

124 "Letter from America to his cousin Count de Kergolay." Extracts: *Memoirs, Lettres, and Remains of Alexis de Tocquevile,* Intra-library loan, courtesy, CUNY Graduate School (New York)

opportunities that included education for all, Alexis de Tocqueville was admittedly dubious about the implementation of such lofty ideals. He hoped that one day freedom, equality and liberty would come to France, yet was it too much to hope for?

19th Century French Women's Fashions

From the earliest of times, ritual dress, costumes and stylish outfits played important roles. In western society, as early as the 18th century, printing presses produced fashion reports. Women pored over fashion magazines.

In France, court customs of the reigning monarchs or leaders of the time usually dictated fashion. One would guess that Mary wore clothes that were contemporary in style, yet were practical and comfortable. Her appearance would have been neat and befitting her lifestyle as chatelaine of the Tocqueville Château.

These were exciting times for women's fashions. The Industrial Revolution with its new spinning machines and looms was producing a diversity of fabrics. Dry goods and other products were more accessible than before.

Dressmakers usually made women's clothing, hiring other seamstresses to help them. Tailors made men's clothing. In 1780 the Duc de Rochefoucauld founded a school for tailors and shoemakers in Liancourt.

Between the years of 1815 and 1830, cotton started to be imported from the United States. Wool came from Normandy and silk from Italy, Lyon and Japan. Lace was imported from England and Belgium. Corduroy was considered a working class fabric.

A trade network developed among the maritime powers of Europe. The textile import-export business became a trade index for domestic business.

Although it's not clear who actually invented the sewing machine, the story behind its development is certainly interesting:

> One of the more reasonable claimants for inventor of the sewing machine must be Barthelemy Thimonnier who, in 1830, was granted a patent by the French government. He used a barbed needle for his machine which was built almost entirely of wood. It is said that he originally designed the machine to do embroidery, but then saw its potential as a sewing machine.
>
> Unlike any others who went before him, he was able to convince the authorities of the usefulness of his invention and he was eventually given a contract to build a batch of machines

and use them to sew uniforms for the French army. In less than 10 years after the granting of his patent Thimonnier had a factory running with 80 machines, but then ran into trouble from Parisian tailors. They feared that, were his machines successful, they would soon take over from hand sewing, putting the craftsmen tailors out of work.

Late one night a group of tailors stormed the factory, destroying every machine, and causing Thimonnier to flee for his life. With a new partner he started again, produced a vastly improved machine and looked set to go into full-scale production; but the tailors attacked again. With France in the grip of revolution, Thimonnier could expect little help from the police or army and fled to England with the one machine he was able to salvage.

He certainly produced the first practical sewing machine, was the first man to offer machines for sale on a commercial basis and ran the first garment factory. For all that, he died in the poor house in 1857...

Perhaps all the essentials of a modern machine came together in early 1844 when Englishman John Fisher invented a machine which although designed for the production of lace, was essentially a working sewing machine. Probably because of miss-filing at the patent office, this invention was overlooked during the long legal arguments between Singer and Howe as to the origins of the sewing machine.

Both Singer and Howe ended their days as multi-millionaires.[125]

Style mattered. Women were convinced that a small waist was worth the pain; their objective was to be *au courant* and attractive, presumably to the opposite sex. Some women became so obsessed with having a small waist, they were laced so tightly they fainted. Sadly, young girls were subjected to "being laced."

[125] http://ismacs.net/sewing_machine_history.html

Often this was a two-hour procedure. Napoleon is quoted as saying, "The corset is the murderer of the human race."

Women's attire included the essentials, one of which was a bonnet. It was thought erotic for a woman to display her hair. The width of the bonnet brims varied, and some were more open than others. Often they were adorned with ribbons or flowers. Like all aspects of dress, they varied with the fashions of the time.

Rubber and elastic were not yet invented, so clothing was held in place by ribbon and cotton ties. The bust line also changed, depending on the period. It was either décolleté or less revealing, using a short cape of transparent material. Waistlines varied and were either higher, lower or at the natural line.

Hairstyles sometimes featured V-shaped partings or hair was worn in tufts following the flaring of the brim. Combs were fashionable, especially those made of tortoise shell. Shoe styles were flat and at one period when skirts were shorter, women wore heel-less slippers. Stockings had open work inserts and other decorative touches.

The cashmere shawl was also important. It was decorative and also served as a coat, providing warmth. At one point, a man's full-skirted double-waisted overcoat was adopted by women who wore it as a lightweight coat that was open at the front. The style originated in England as a riding habit.

In general, available materials were silk, wool, cashmere and cotton. Style was influenced by events in France and England, but ultimately France became the leader. Fashion was mainly for the higher levels of society, since the lower classes would have been unable to afford such expensive items. Moreover, they would have had little or no use for a closet filled with elaborate garments. Where would they have worn them, and for whom to admire?

Haute couture remained the prerequisite of the aristocracy, the *noblesse oblige* since their lives revolved around soirees, balls, receptions, the races and theater. These were the women who formed the customer base for the House of Worth. Charles Frederick Worth, an English designer, established himself in Paris and very quickly attracted the aristocratic ladies, who flocked to his salon. Gowns often cost thousands of francs.

Closely following behind the aristocracy was the emergence of the *haute bourgeois.* Middle class women, whose lives revolved around their homes and children, were also expected to look beautiful and well dressed, but they had to be careful not to dress in styles that could best be described as erotic; they couldn't risk being thought of as *avant garde.* However, as a group, these women were becoming increasingly influential, demanding choice and exerting their purchasing power.

City fashion differed from fashion in smaller towns. Economics played a large role in choice. The average bourgeois women living more traditional lives in the home favored the more conservative and practical styles, in keeping with their role as homemaker. Peasant women who lived in the countryside on farms, working in the fields with crops and animals may have been interested in fashion, but they made more practical choices. It is unlikely that they owned more than two dresses: one for daily wear and one for church on Sunday.

Mary came from a prominent bourgeois family in Portsmouth, England. Many of these people were financially secure and could not be described as being poor or of low birth, so they must have been well aware of *haute couture.*

Alexis and Mary were married during the reign of Louis-Phillippe, when fashions were soft and relaxed. Hair was dressed in bands with chignons and long ringlets. The pattern was simple with Bertha collars that covered the shoulders. Floor length flounced skirts were coming into vogue. Ball gowns at that time were made of light materials, with full sleeves and an oval neckline exposing the shoulders.

Bonnets replaced hats and cashmere scarves were longer, serving as coats. It is unlikely that Mary had need of ball gowns, since she had no desire to be part of a society that shunned her. In the portrait of Mary at the Château de Tocqueville, which is on the front cover of this book, she is wearing a dress of soft material and the Bertha collar is tied at the neck with a bow. Her hair appears to be naturally curly. It frames her face and she is wearing a comb that is fastened on the crown of her head.

It is interesting to consider how clothes were laundered during the 19th century. The aristocratic ladies surely had maids who must have faced multiple challenges with the lace, silk and satin gowns. The simple dress Mary is wearing in the portrait suggests that it would have been easier to launder.

When Alexis visited America in 1831, he marveled at the fact that American women wore the same dress from morning until evening. As an aristocrat, it was his experience that ladies changed their outfits several times throughout the day, and again in the evening.

The Industrial Revolution

By the end of the 19th century, technological advancements were rapidly transforming European and American life. With the advent of the printing press came the world of commercialism and the birth of marketing and advertising. Traveling salesmen made shopping easier and department stores started to appear in the larger towns. One can imagine the excitement and sense of victory the women must have felt when shopping in a department store for the first time.

Above all, women's suffrage and improvements in education would be the big game changers. When mainstream Europe and America finally conceded that women's brains were not smaller than men's after all and that both sexes had the same intellectual capabilities, life changed dramatically.

Neither Mary nor Alexis lived long enough to witness these radical changes. Surely their lives would have been altogether different, yet under other circumstances perhaps they may never have met.

CERTIFIED COPY OF AN ENTRY OF DEATH

GIVEN AT THE GENERAL REGISTER OFFICE

Application Number Y544193

REGISTRATION DISTRICT Portsea Island

1863 DEATH in the Sub-district of Sandport in the County of Southampton

Columns:–	1	2	3	4	5	6	7	8	9
No.	When and where died	Name and surname	Sex	Age	Occupation	Cause of death	Signature, description and residence of informant	When registered	Signature of registrar
[illegible]	[illegible] January 1863 [illegible]	Mary Mottley	Female	89 years	[illegible]	[illegible]	[illegible]	[illegible] January 1863	[illegible]

CERTIFIED to be a true copy of an entry in the certified copy of a Register of Deaths in the District above mentioned.

Given at the GENERAL REGISTER OFFICE, under the Seal of the said Office, the 3rd day of December 2003

DYA 237627

See note overleaf

CAUTION: THERE ARE OFFENCES RELATING TO FALSIFYING OR ALTERING A CERTIFICATE AND USING OR POSSESSING A FALSE CERTIFICATE ©CROWN COPYRIGHT

WARNING: A CERTIFICATE IS NOT EVIDENCE OF IDENTITY.

Mary Mottley's Death Certificate

9

Excerpts of Alexis de Tocqueville's Letters to Mary Mottley

The following chapter consists of a selection of letters written by Alexis de Tocqueville to Mary Mottley, Madame Marie de Tocqueville, his wife.

Through Alexis's words we have sufficient validation of what I could only have assumed: that he loved his wife passionately and he was very devoted to her throughout their marriage.

The letters are translated by Claudine Martin-Yurth, who was born in Normandy, France. Claudine also came to the US as an adult and eventually became a US citizen. I am grateful to her for this major contribution to the book.

Both Claudine and I are extremely grateful to Dr. Jean-Louis Benoît for referring us to his work, *Oeuvres Completes, Tome XIV: Correspondance Familiale*[126], in which these letters appear.

Translator's Note: In his preface, Jean-Louis Benoît identifies several topics which are found in the letters to Marie Mottley: his immense love for her, her role in managing the couple's finances and property, and her influence in his political carrier. I have included samples of each of these topics. I also selected a particular letter which shows some of the hostility from his family toward her.

---

[126] Benoît, Jean-Louis, *Oeuvres complètes, tome 14: Correspondance familiale [Volume XIV, Family Correspondence,* Gallimard (24 mars 1998)], Dr. Benoît's comprehensive work about Alexis de Tocqueville, http://www.amazon.fr/Alexis-Tocqueville-compl%C3%A8tes-Correspondance-familiale/dp/2070750655/ref=sr_1_16?ie=UTF8&qid=1439991737&sr=8-16&keywords=jean-louis+benoit, Translated with the permission of Gallimard

Whenever necessary to provide reference or clarification within the context of the letter, I have included the translation of J. L. Benoît's footnotes.

Letter 76M, page 485 of CORRESPONDANCE FAMILIALE

August 8, 1844, this Thursday morning

I love you with all my heart, however I must tell you without delay that surely you are the most insane creature living under the sun. How could you torment yourself, as you told me last Monday, in the letter I just received? To imagine that I don't love you, that I love you just a little or less, as you do every moment and to torment your own body and soul with these thoughts for no reason, truly this is insane. This is like covering your eyes with your own hands and declaring that daylight doesn't exist. What bond in the world can be compared to the one that unites us? I'm asking you. And if I did not love you with all my heart wouldn't it be enough to become violently angry when at the slightest incident, at the slightest slip of my mind due to my diseased condition, what else can I say, when the slightest cloud invades your mind, anything is enough to hide for you sixteen years of tender, devoted love, of growing trust, of mutual attraction which grows more intense every year? Admit it, you are insane, but an insane person I wouldn't trade for all of Solomon's wisdom because, in spite of all your thoughts regarding me and all the chagrin they often cause me, I persist in saying that more and more I don't trust anyone in the world like I trust you, I don't feel real intimacy with anyone else; that you alone possess the key to my soul and that without you, truly, I wouldn't want to live. Without you the world would be a desert where I would find myself as isolated as the first man. In there, no one would speak my language, and I would be forced to live face to face with just myself. I pray you, for God's sake, do not believe that such a feeling which has been pushing its roots for nearly twenty years into the deepest parts of my being, which has become so much part of my soul that from now on it couldn't be torn out even if I wanted to, do not believe that such a feeling is at the mercy of small daily incidents. No, no, you must believe that it will only leave me with my own life and with every year its power grows more intense. You are the heiress to everything, Marie, can't you see? Don't you see that this need for attachment, confidence, intimacy that my youth delighted in pouring into the heart of relatives and friends is more and more turning toward you only and you are rewarded with everything they have lost?

Your letter is the cause of this impetuous outpouring of thoughts from my soul. However I don't want to end this letter without a word about my situation and the state of our affairs. The violent crisis, in the midst of it I was writing to you yesterday is over. After a long interview between me and Scheffer,[127] we came

[127] Scheffer's articles enraged his old friend Corcelle, who had brought him to be the chief editor of the *Commerce*. Tocqueville must have spoken in favor of him even though he was aware of his limitations. Later on, Scheffer

to the decision that we will keep him. I could write volumes to explain to you why, I will tell you later. I think that we have nothing to fear now in regard with his eccentric outbursts which were so scary for us. Yet, the man's abilities remain quite poor and all he brings to the newspaper is the strength of his well-deserved and excellent reputation.

To cut him would have caused serious consequences: first to trigger a public explanation between us; second, it would have forced us to stay here indefinitely, until we would have created new instruments. This last consideration was all I needed to make my decision. Such a sacrifice was more than I could bear. Because I don't have to tell you I am consumed with the desire to leave. However, I am still obliged to stay here a few more days to put everything into motion. If you want to know what my life is like: it is the life of the most miserable devil of a journalist. I work all day long, I have dinner with Corcelle. From there we

gave up his position as editor for the newspaper, while keeping some kind of authority role in the team.

go to the newspaper where we stay until midnight or one in the morning to start all over again the next day. It's a monk's life in the midst of the turmoil of this big city...

Letter 69M, page 474 of CORRESPONDANCE FAMILIALE

Saint-Lô, this Tuesday morning [August 24, 1843]

Your first letter, which I was so impatient to receive, came yesterday, my friend, my tender and only friend. How can I tell you all the emotions it stirred in me. If speaking is often powerless to express the most sincere, most intense feelings of the heart, writing is a thousand times worse. I am so grateful for this letter! It soothed my soul's extreme bitterness. It gave me courage. You are an angel, Marie, an angel of kindness, purity, elevation. May God at last grant me the power to be worthy of you! But what touched me the most in your letter, what penetrated me instantly deep into my bone marrow, is the tenderness, the extreme and touching tenderness which vibrates in every sentence. Oh! How could I ever complain about my destiny as long as this immense wealth is in my possession! I will not tell you, my friend, that on my side, I love you beyond and above all things. Because you must know it, and if you had any doubt, a few worthless words scribbled on the paper would be unable to bring in your heart a certitude that my speech and all my actions were unable to give you. But this certitude, Marie, you have it. How could you not have it? How could this indescribable tenderness which fills my heart, my anxiety about all that concerns you, this sweet gratitude (because it is so sweet to owe everything to the one we love) that I feel every time I think of the happiness I owe to you, this terror that invades me from top to bottom every time I think I could lose you, all these feelings, Marie, which so often disturb my soul when I think about you and when I am in your beloved presence, all these feelings cannot hide; the least trained eye is witness to the proof they exist and I challenge you to ignore them. These feelings are a thousand times deeper and sharper than I can express and yet I am constantly hurting you; I often hurt a heart who lives just for me. When I think of this, Marie, I hold myself in horror. I don't know how to avoid the poignant pain that tears my soul apart. I know, my beloved friend, I have no right to affirm I will never hurt you again. So often in my life, have I committed this inexcusable mistake that I have no more promises to give.[128]

However, either I know myself very poorly, or I am unable to distinguish in my soul between what is real and deep and what is superficial and temporary, or if I affirm that I will not cause you any chagrin anymore. You will see, Marie, I can only appeal to experience itself.

---

[128] In the letter written from Paris a year ago, it can be felt that Tocqueville is trying to deny his faults in front of Marie's jealousy by trying to make multiple assurances, showing that his life in Paris is boring, laborious, without social activities. In this letter, the situation is much clearer: Tocqueville admits to his frequent infidelities.

I arrived here the evening before last. I found right away a great room, very clean where I am comfortable. Yesterday, we had our first meeting at the Conseil Général. Having got elected, by a three vote majority only, and he owes them to me, because not only did I turn them down, but I asked my friends to vote for him. Today, we are beginning to work seriously. I want to be involved as much as possible. My wish here is to realize your desire. You tell me you have always wanted to make me happy and great. You have already made me happy more than any other woman could have done, as much as my nature could allow. And, if one day I reach greatness, which I am not aware I ever will, God alone will know himself how much this would have been thanks to you.

I am sending this letter through the normal route. But, from now on, I will send all my letters through Barfleur. This way, if you send someone for them, you will have them in the evening instead of the next morning. As you know, the office is at Despointes'. I will always place my letters in an envelope and I will seal them with wax and my own stamp. Do the same thing. Your last letter was not stamped on the wax. Use your own little stamp. That way I assure you, we will have nothing to fear from the post office. So let us speak with open heart in our letters and let us not worsen the cruel pain caused by being apart with the strain on two beings so tenderly united of not speaking openly. I need your letters. I need to receive them very often. I need them to keep me from falling into depression and sorrow. I need them to be able to work and push forward. Think, Marie, that you hold my destiny in your hands. You can make me the most unfortunate among all men or grant me all the happiness God has allowed me to have in this world. If you would withdraw your heart from me, I would cease doing anything and desiring anything. Farewell, my beloved friend, farewell you whom I adore, please remind me to your brothers.

Alexis

Letters from Alexis to Mary

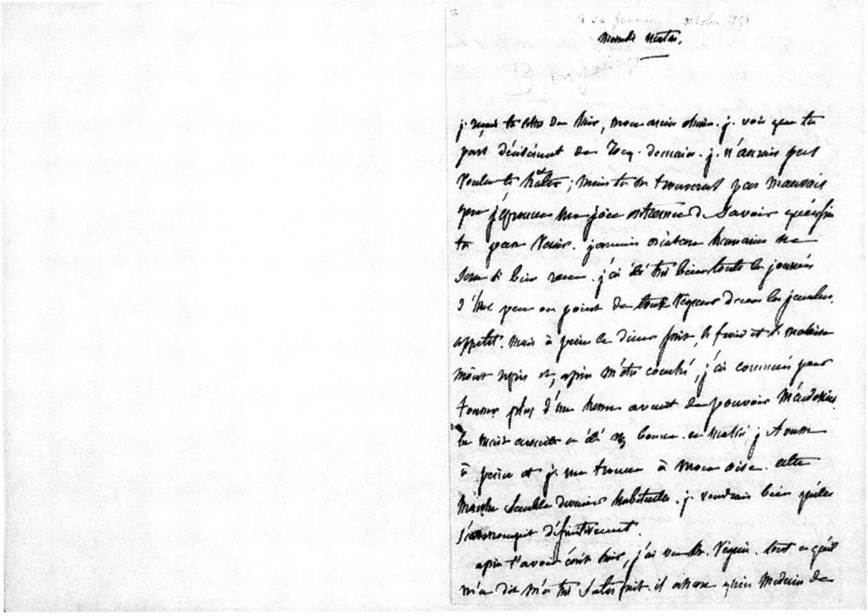

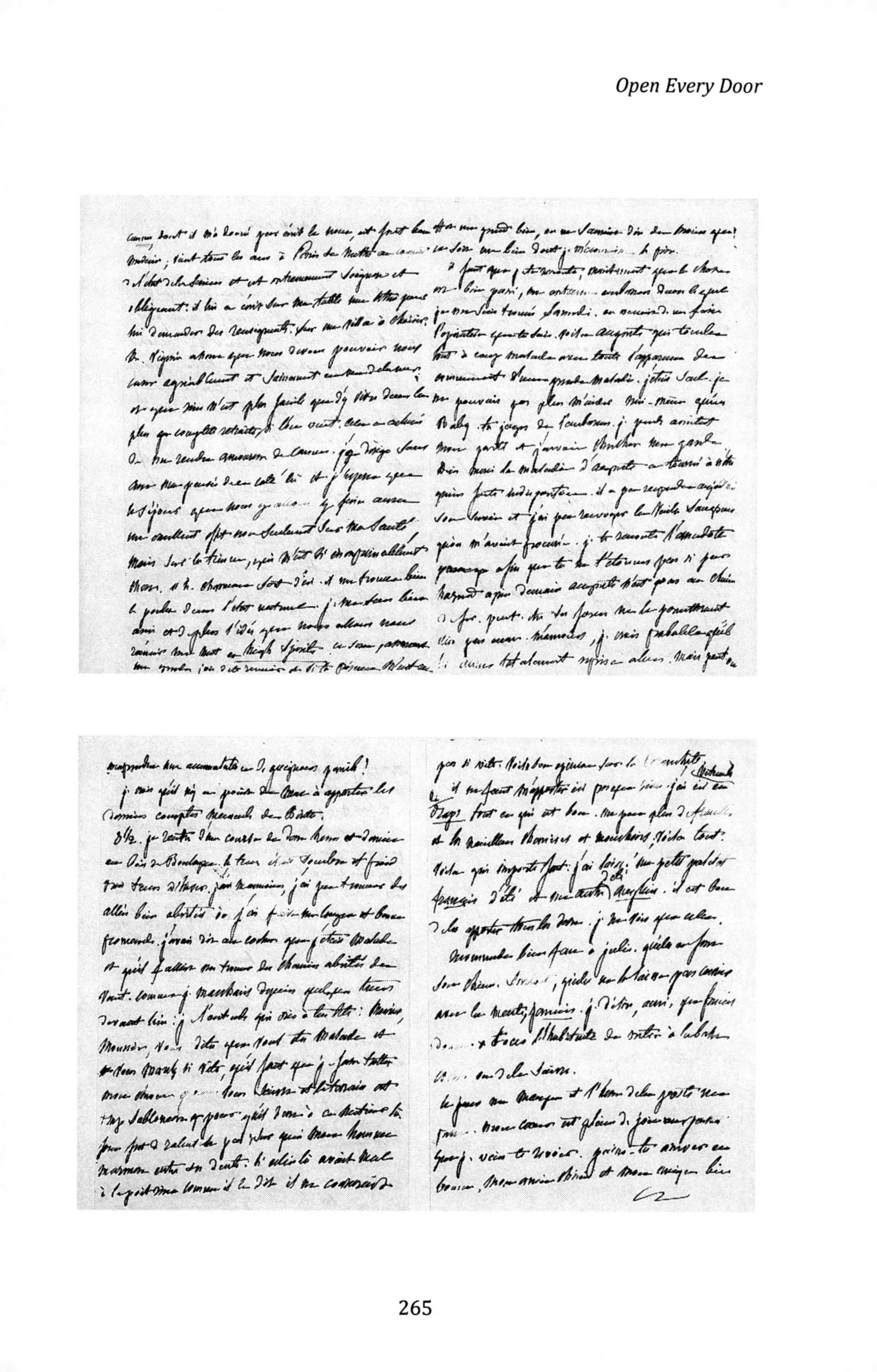

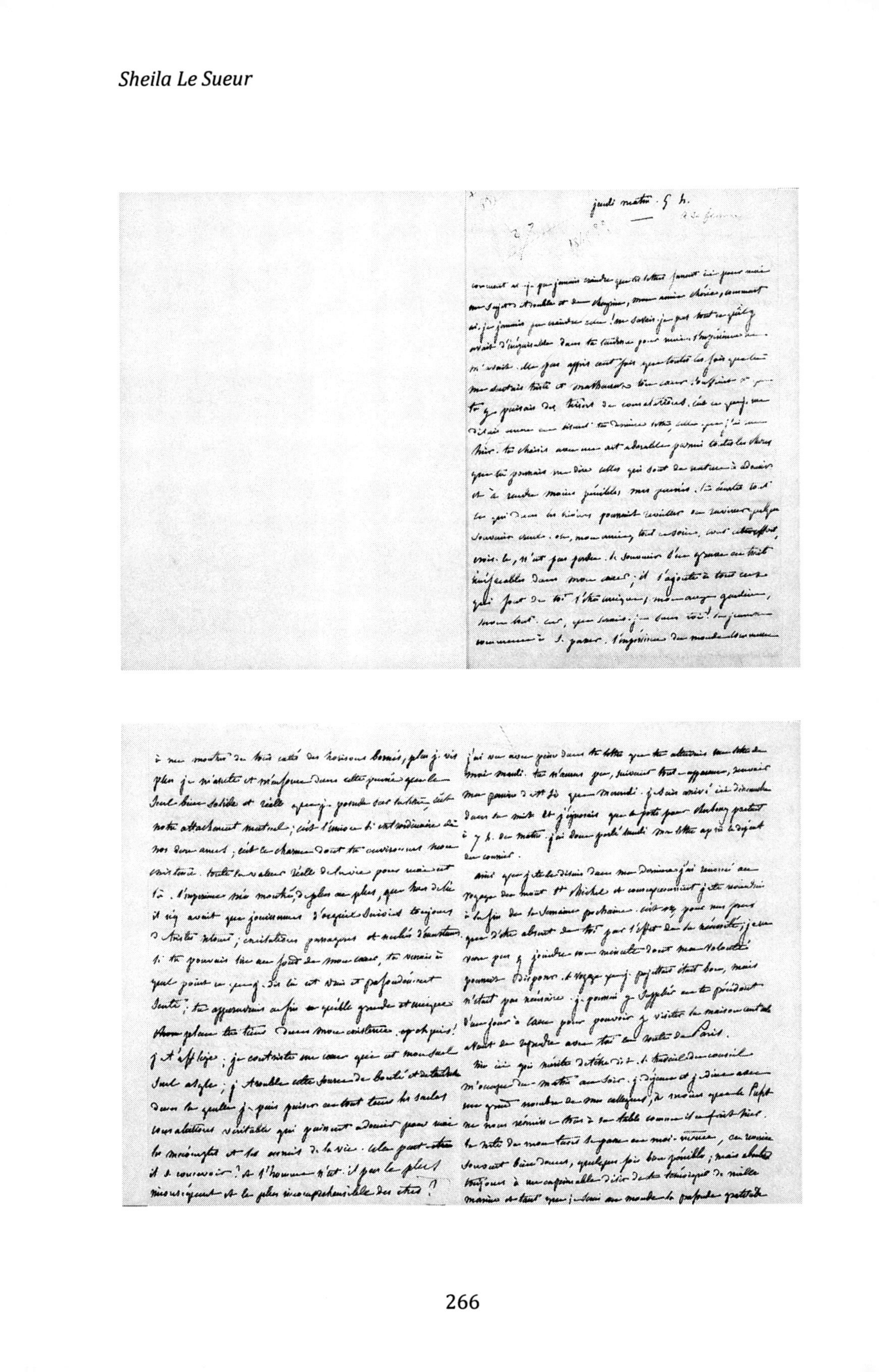

et la tendresse infinie que j'ai pour toi. Marie, mon amie chérie, mon unique amie, mon seul bien véritable, conserve-moi le cœur sans lequel je ne puis vivre et mes chances de bonheur au lieu de diminuer croîtront avec les années, car chaque année m'a fait sentir plus vivement ton prix.

Je te quitte pour me livrer à la seule distraction que je puisse avoir au travail. Continue à m'écrire de ces adorables lettres qui me donnent du courage. Aime-moi et pense sans cesse que tu tiens ma destinée dans tes mains. Je te donne mille fois tout mon cœur. Je suis triste en pensant qu'il faut maintenant attendre 30 heures pour recevoir ta chère écriture

[illegible]

1 Jeudi matin 5h.

Comment ai-je pu jamais craindre que tes lettres fussent ici pour moi un sujet de trouble et de chagrin, mon amie chérie, comment ai-je jamais pu craindre cela? Ne savais-je pas tout ce qu'il y avait d'inépuisable dans ta tendresse pour moi. L'expérience ne m'avait-elle pas appris cent fois que toutes les fois que tu me sentais triste et malheureux ton coeur souffrait et que tu y puisais des trésors de consolations. C'est ce que je me disais encore en lisant ta dernière lettre, celle que j'ai reçu hier. Tu choisis avec un art adorable parmi toutes les choses que tu pourrais me dire celles qui sont de nature à adoucir et à rendre moins pénibles mes pensées. Tu écartes tout ce qui dans les termes pourraient réveiller ou raviver quelque souvenir cruel. Oh, mon amie, tout ce soin, tout cet effort crois-le, n'est pas perdu. Le souvenir s'en grave en traits ineffaçables dans mon coeur; il s'ajoute à tous ceux qui font de toi l'être unique, mon ange gardien, mon tout. Car, que serais-je sans toi? La jeunesse commence à se passer. L'expérience du monde commence à me montrer de tous côtés des horizons bornés; plus je vis, plus je m'arrête et m'enfonce dans cette pensée que le seul bien solide et réel que je possède sur la terre, c'est notre attachement

2

mutuel ; c'est l'union si extraordinaire de nos deux âmes, c'est le charme dont tu environnes mon existence. Toute la valeur réelle de la vie pour moi est là. L'expérience m'a montré de plus en plus, que hors de là il n'y avait que jouissances d'orgueil suivies toujours de tristes retours ; excitations passagères et mêlées d'amertume. Si tu pouvais lire au fond de mon cœur, tu verrais à quel point ce que je dis là est vrai et profondément senti ; tu apercevrais enfin quelle grande et unique place tu tiens dans mon existence. Et puis ! je t'afflige ; je contriste un cœur qui est mon seul asile ; je trouble cette source de bonté et de tendresse (asyle) dans laquelle je puis puiser en tous temps les seules consolations véritables qui puissent adoucir pour moi les mécomptes et les ennuis de la vie. Cela peut-il se concevoir ? et l'homme n'est-il pas le plus inconséquent et le plus incompréhensible des êtres ?

J'ai vu avec peine dans ta lettre que tu attendais une lettre de moi mardi. Tu n'auras pu, suivant toute apparence, recevoir ma première de St Lô que mercredi. Je suis arrivé ici dimanche dans la nuit et j'ignorais que la poste pour Cherbourg partait à 7 h. du matin. J'ai donc porté lundi ma lettre après le départ du courrier.

3

Ainsi que je te le disais dans ma dernière j'ai renoncé au voyage du Mont St Michel et conséquemment je te reviendrai à la fin de la semaine prochaine. C'est assez pour mes forces que d'être absent de toi par l'effet de la nécessité, je ne veux pas y joindre une minute dont ma volonté pourrait disposer. Le voyage que je projetais était bon, mais n'était pas nécessaire. Je pourrai y suppléer en te précédant d'un jour à Caen pour pouvoir y visiter la maison centrale avant de reprendre avec toi la route de Paris.

Rien ici qui mérite de t'être dit. Le travail du conseil m'occupe du matin au soir. Je déjeune et je dîne avec un grand nombre de mes collègues, à moins que le Préfet ne nous réunissent tous à sa table comme il a fait hier. Le reste de mon temps se passe en moi-même, en rêveries souvent bien douces, quelquefois bien pénibles, mais aboutissant toujours à un inséparable désir de te témoigner de mille manières et tant que je serai au monde la profonde gratitude et la tendresse infinie que j'ai pour toi. Marie, mon amie chérie, mon unique amie, mon seul bien véritable, conserve-moi ce cœur sans lequel je ne puis vivre et nos chances de bonheur au lieu de diminuer croîtront avec les années, car chaque année m'a fait sentir plus vivement ton prix.

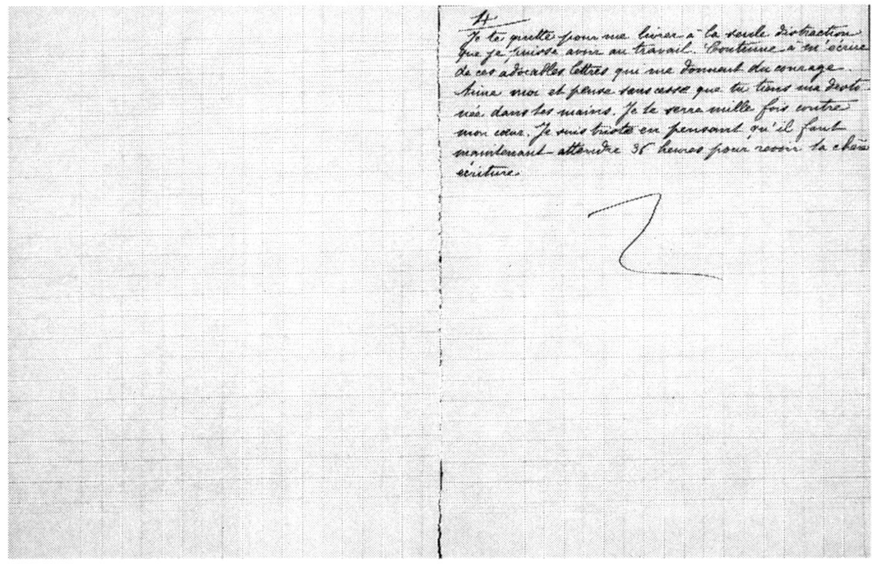

4

Je te quitte pour me livrer à la seule distraction
que je puisse avoir au travail. Continue à m'écrire
de ces adorables lettres qui me donnent du courage.
Aime moi et pense sans cesse que tu tiens ma destinée dans tes mains. Je te serre mille fois contre
mon cœur. Je suis triste en pensant qu'il faut
maintenant attendre 36 heures pour revoir ta chère
écriture.

Letter 19M, extract, page 399 of CORRESPONDANCE FAMILIALE

[circa 1835]

...I have never been able to divide the world in more than two parts: on the one hand, action, noise, reputation—it's the external world; on the other hand, the heart's sweet emotions, the sharing of every feeling, of every thought—here, I see only you, I have never met anyone else but you. You are the only one who embodies this enchanted portion of life in my imagination.

The only one who ever will. Marie, I repeat again what I said earlier: we are linked together *in life and in death*. Believe me, no one ever feels twice in life what I have been feeling for you for several years. I thought I was in love twelve years ago, but if you could see how little the sentiment you inspire me now resembles what I felt then, indeed you would notice that love then was in my imagination and is now in my heart. I have trouble using the word "love" to speak of the sentiment we share together. It is said that love is a temporary feeling and what I feel for you can't be altered by time...

Letter 25M, page 410 of CORRESPONDANCE FAMILIALE

Paris, Tuesday [December 26, 1837], 2 pm

Even though I wrote to you this morning, I want to do it again. I just received the letter you sent yesterday. It moved me, touched me and elevated my heart. For it is admirable. It will remain apart in my correspondence with you as one of these letters which best portray you and best justify in my eyes my unlimited attachment to you. Why don't you always write to me in this style, so clear, so simple, revealing so well such exquisite sentiments and such noble thoughts? Also, this letter proves to me more and more, that only misunderstandings stand between us now and then.

Let me reply to you with the simplicity and truthfulness you yourself give me the example here.

You believe that I blamed you for having bad feelings toward my family. Not at all. It's a complete nonsense. It's was only toward me that recently I felt little kindness from you. You make judgments regarding my father, Edouard and Alexandrine to which I have nothing to add or remove. They are correct, I know that better than anyone else. Like you, I love Alexandrine dearly, and she irritates me to the point that makes me grouchy with her. Like you, I think her soul is enclosed inside a small circle beyond which your soul spreads and elevates itself infinitely, and consequently I know very well that even though you two have a strong attraction for each other, you are not made to live together, permanently under the same roof. I know all that; when you say these things, my mind is in total agreement with yours. Far from condemning you, I agree with you. I can see clearly the point where your mind stops. This satisfies me and I want nothing else. But when you express some vague criticism, I fear the presence in your soul of more causes for irritation, greater than I had imagined before; hence the source of my worries which from then on are irritating for you. Let's commit to always speak to each other with openness and express without cover just what we want to say.

There's only one place in your letter where I don't agree with you. It's where you say that my family views my behavior with sadness and that they accuse you of influencing it.[129]

I must admit I don't see enough proof of these two statements, especially the second one. Nothing, either directly or indirectly, has happened to me until now which would make me believe that. But let's talk about it later.

You are quite right to feel affectionate for my father. Because he loves you very tenderly. Yesterday, he wrote me a long letter to pull me out of the melancholic state which you told him I was in; and the first motive he gave me to show me the beauty of life was you. It was to have you with me.

I am running out of time and the turmoil in which your letter threw me is not helping me to gather my ideas, but I will find

[129] It is true that the political choices made by Tocqueville were to become totally incompatible with his family's. It is equally true that the marriage of Tocqueville with Marie was never totally accepted by Alexis' family.

myself more at ease with my feelings, and I will not have to search anywhere to tell you that my heart is full of you, that I am deeply touched by your letter, that I love you with all my soul, with all my strength. That I honor you as much as I love you; you are the one I always knew you were. My real and only friend, my companion; the only soul in the world capable of completely hearing and feeling mine, capable of supporting and sustaining me through the carrier glorious maybe, undoubtedly stormy, which the future holds for me. I am dying with the need to see you again. I am counting the days still separating me from you. Oh! My beloved friend, we can still be happy together. Two beings who love each other like we do always have happiness within their reach, if they will grab it.

Farewell, I must leave you...

A.

Letter 6M, page 379 of CORRESPONDANCE FAMILIALE

[From America, 1831-1832][130]

...And what could I blame you for? For introducing me to the only real happiness I ever tasted in the world, for reviving greatly my interest in this existence, for enduring without complaint the violent and arbitrary nature of my character, for conquering me with the power of your sweet and tender nature? To my knowledge these are the only crimes I can blame you for. You have done even more for me, my beloved friend, and I saved this benefit for the last one to mention. You pulled me away from a path where without you I would have probably lost myself. You made me savor for the first time, the noble, generous and let me say virtuous aspect of real love. I declare it to you that I believe my love for you makes me a better person. I love all that is good more for the love of you than for any other reason. At the very thought of you I feel my soul being elevated; I would like to

[130] During Tocqueville's trip to America, Ernest de Chabrol continued to live in the apartment on Rue d'Anjou, that they had been renting together and he became the "mailbox" which allowed Alexis' mail to reach Marie.

make you proud of me and prove to you every day that you were not mistaken in your choice. Finally I never feel more inclined to think about God, more convinced of the reality of an afterlife than when I think of you. You may have noticed the peculiar pleasure with which I enjoyed discussing with you the most serious topics regarding life. Only you in the world, *without a single exception*, are familiar with the beliefs about these topics that are hidden in the deepest part of my soul; only you are aware of my instincts, my hopes, my doubts. If I am ever converted to Christianity, I believe it will be thanks to you. What I'm saying here, Marie, isn't something I just thought about today...

Haven't you noticed, my tender friend, that our happiest moments happened when we hardly spoke. I have often thought that in these instants our two souls were communicating with each other without using the senses, like some people say it happens after death. Each one of us was enjoying one's own happiness and the other's happiness; our perceptions, our feelings, our ideas, were exchanged from one soul to the other a thousand times faster than with words, and yet the deepest silence reigned between us. How could anyone who has never loved comprehend such pleasures? How could anyone ever forget them who has felt them once? For me, if I were ever so unfortunate to die before seeing you again, my beloved friend, what I would miss about life, wouldn't be the pleasures to which almost all men get attached, no I swear, my only desperate regret would be to not be able anymore to feel love's sweet sorrow, to not be able to hear the inside voice of the soul. I would miss not the worldly pleasures but the very chagrin of a heart that is in love and even the sweet sighs it exhales...

I love like I've never loved before in my life. My mind and my heart adore you equally. My love didn't happen suddenly: you earned it little by little as every day you revealed more of yourself to me. You conquered it, you possess it entirely: you reign over my soul now as an absolute monarch. I don't love you with the love of a sixteen year old, and yet at the very thought of you, I feel all the generous passions, all the noble instincts, the total detachment from the self which ordinarily happens at this age only...

I don't know why, Marie, men are created with such a variety of types. Some seek only pleasures in life, others only pain. Some view the world as a ballroom, and for me I am always inclined to view it as a battlefield where everyone shows up in turn to fight, be wounded and die. It is at the bottom of this somber imagination that most of the violent passions that often disturb me are almost always created. If sometimes it causes grief to some people, it gives me plenty. But I believe, I truly believe that it gives me an energy for loving that other men don't possess...

Letter 42M, page 439 of CORRESPONDANCE FAMILIALE

Paris, June 21 [1841]

I just arrived in Paris, my beloved little wife, in very good health, except for a remnant of weakness. The two days I spent in Lyon to get some rest did wonders. There the diarrhea finally bid me farewell for the last time. Since then, that's three days ago, I'm able to eat, which pleases me greatly, because I enjoy an all-consuming appetite and consequently my strength is visibly coming back. I feel myself rejuvenated for good and I begin to hope that this horrible crisis will not have the long and annoying effects I feared. However, my satisfaction is far from turning into joy.

I found here two of your letters, my beloved little wife, one dated June 18, the other June 20. The report you give me about our financial situation upsets me. I can see that as always we ran out of money.[131]

This made me decide against the purchase of books, which was not necessary anyway. I am coming back with four hundred and fifty francs; the Académie will pay me at least two hundred. Therefore I'll be able to pay Desmartins five hundred.[132]

Moreover, I'll sell our bank action. Finally, I'll take care without delay of the important deal you mentioned regarding a lost financial security. For now it doesn't make any sense to me. We've never paid any money if I'm not mistaken; how could we hold a security in our hands? You recommend I read your answer to Desmartins and you didn't send me a copy. How could I fulfill your request?

---

[131] Marie was, according to Tocqueville, the couple's "Minister of Finances." Their financial situation was then gravely affected by the two renovation projects of the Château [1839 and 1840] and his trip to Algeria, which was ending at that time.

[132] Desmartins was Tocqueville's business man in Paris.

Altogether, all the troubles and frustrations you tell me you had since I left also sadden me. You should have either not mentioned them or given me more details; without either one, my mind keeps going painfully over the matter. What kind of huge frustration did you have to suffer? You seem to attach too great an investment in having Tocqueville ready for my return. If only you knew how little I care about this and how what I look for at Tocqueville is something other than an orderly castle. If indeed this is the main cause of your discomfort, you are quite wrong. Upon my arrival here, I found another cause of concern needing my attention. The academician Monsieur de Cessac passed away, and this opens a seat at the moral sciences department for Beaumont and one for me at the Académie Française. The elections will not happen for several months. But the deal must be closed now as they say. The resting period I've been looking for, for two weeks, will now be spent paying visits, some to the ministers, some to the academicians. It makes me furious in advance. I figure that no matter how diligent I am and how eager I am to get out of here, I won't be able to get on the road before Saturday 26, in the evening. Therefore you still have time to write to me and you would please me greatly if you did. Peace and contentment, Marie, are only on your side, you know it well and you do notice. I feel an indescribable urge to talk with you. I don't know how your last letters didn't seem to me as tender as ordinarily; it saddened me. Could there be in your mind some sort of cloud against me, some drop of bitterness at the bottom of your heart that you don't want to share with me? In God's name, where could this come from? If, with all the feelings I have for you, I can't plainly satisfy your heart, indeed, I must forever renounce the idea that I'll ever be able to do it. In the end it may be just a remnant of my somber state of mind. Because, as I told you earlier, it has not been cleared yet. The fact is that I arrived in Paris this morning, and I'm already bored here and wishing I was leaving. The work I have to do here is disgusting to me in advance. Fortunately, as you say, I am *elastic*...

Letter 71M, page 478 of CORRESPONDANCE FAMILIALE

Thursday, 5am [August 26, 1843 ?]

How could I ever fear that your letters could be for me a source of trouble and chagrin, my beloved friend, how could I ever be afraid of that? Didn't I know the inexhaustible nature of your tenderness for me? Didn't experience teach me a hundred times that every time you felt me to be sad and unhappy your heart suffered and from there would come an outpouring wealth of comforting words? Once again, I noticed that as I was reading your last letter, the one I received yesterday. Among all the things you could tell me, you have an adorable way to select the ones which by nature are able to soothe and soften my thoughts. You avoid every one of yours that could awaken or revive a cruel memory. Oh! my friend, all this care, all this effort, believe me, is not in vain. It leaves an indestructible memory engraved in my heart; and with all the other ones it makes you the only being, my guardian angel, my whole. For what would I be without you?

My youth is beginning to fade away. My experience of the world begins to show avenues going nowhere all around me, the more I advance in life the more I pause and sink myself in the knowledge that my only solid and true possession on earth is our mutual attachment; the union ever so extraordinary of our two souls; the enchanted environment you create in my existence. The entire real value of life for me is right there. More and more, experience proves to me, that on the outside of this reality is found only the pleasures of vanity which bring always sad returns; temporary excitements mixed with bitterness. If you could read the bottom of my heart, you would see to what extent what I'm telling you is true and deeply felt; at last, you would be aware of what a huge and unique place you occupy in my life. And then! I hurt you; I sadden a heart which is my only refuge; I spoil the source of gentleness and tenderness where at any time I can find the only true consolation capable of softening for me the miscalculations and annoyances of life. How can this be? And isn't man the most unreliable and incomprehensible of all creatures? I saw with sorrow in your letter that you were expecting a letter from me on Tuesday. In all probabilities, you could only receive the first one I sent from Saint-Lô on Wednesday. I arrived here on Sunday, during the night and I didn't know that the mail left for Cherbourg at 7 o'clock in the morning. Therefore I brought my letter to the post-office after the mail had left...

...Marie, my beloved friend, my sole friend, my only authentic wealth, save for me the heart without which I cannot live, and our chance of happiness instead of decreasing will grow with time, because with every year passing I feel more acutely how precious you are to me.

I leave you to engage in the only entertainment I have at work. Keep writing to me these adorable letters which give me courage. Love me and know at every moment that you hold my destiny in your hands. I hug you a thousand times against my chest. I'm sad thinking that I will have to wait now thirty-six hours until I can see again your beloved hand-writing.

A.

Letter 207M, page 666 of CORRESPONDANCE FAMILIALE

Wednesday morning [October 6 1858]

I just received the letter you sent yesterday, my beloved friend. I see that you decided to leave Tocqueville tomorrow. I did not want to pressure you; but you will not find unpleasant that I am extremely overjoyed to know that finally you're able to come. Never, has a human creature been welcome as you will be. I felt really well all day, yesterday. A little or no cough. My legs feeling strong. A good appetite. But as soon as dinner was ready, the chills and nausea came back, and once in bed, I started coughing again for over one hour before falling asleep. The rest of the night was fairly good. This morning, I'm barely coughing, and feeling comfortable. This course of events is turning into a habit. I wish it would stop definitively.

After I wrote to you yesterday, I saw Monsieur Vignier. Everything he told me was very satisfying to me. He is sure that a doctor in Cannes, whose name he wrote down for me, is a very good doctor; every year he comes to Paris to be updated with what's new in science and he is very meticulous and obliging. He wrote him a letter on my table asking him some information about a villa to rent. Monsieur Vignier is sure that we should be able to settle in a place overlooking the sea which will be pleasant and healthy for us. And that nothing is easier than to live there in complete seclusion, if you want to. All that helped me finally fall in love with Cannes. My thoughts keep going there and I hope that the time we're going to spend there will have an excellent effect not only on my health, but on yours too, which is dear to me beyond words.

...

Three and a half hour o'clock

I just got home after a two-and-a-half hour walk in the bois de Boulogne. The weather was gray and cold, a real winter day. Nevertheless, I was able to find some well sheltered alleys where I did a long and good walk. I had told the coachman that I was sick and he had to take me to some trails well sheltered from the wind. As I had walked for some time in front of him, I heard him shouting at the top of his voice: "Sir, Sir, you told me you're sick and you're walking so fast I have to make my horse trot to follow you and it is too sandy here to have him go on like this." I had to slow down; then I heard the fellow mumble in his teeth: "If this one really had so much pain in his chest as he's saying, he wouldn't run so fast." That's what he thinks about bronchitis.

I almost don't need you to bring me anything here. All the suits I have here are fine. Some more flannels and my best shirts and handkerchiefs, that's all. Here something very important: I left a little French summer coat and another English summer coat. It would be good to bring them both. That's all I see.

...

The day is coming to the end and I must hurry before the post office closes. My heart is filled with joy at the thought of seeing you again. May you arrive in good health, my beloved friend and my only wealth. Al.[133]

---

[133] This letter is the last one Tocqueville sent to Marie before their departure to Cannes, where he was to succumb after a short coma on April 16 1859. Until the end of February, as shown in his correspondence with his brother Edouard and his nephew Hubert, Tocqueville believed he was on his way to get well when at the same time the doctors knew he was dying.

Conclusion

Even if limited by a world that had not yet witnessed all the modern conveniences of transportation and communication, even if condemned by her husband's family for no other crime than that of being born into the wrong class, and even if all women were considered merely chattel or material property, Mary Mottley/Mme. Marie de Tocqueville refused to be a victim.

In fact, she must have considered herself luckier than most to be married to a man who dearly loved and valued her for her mind as well as her wit.

Ironically, Mary was probably more liberated than most because she refused to allow herself to get upset about other people's opinions of her. By transcending their pettiness and jealousy, she proved that she was a Woman for All Time whose life story deserved to be placed next to her famous husband's in the Universal Hall of Fame. In this book, we have set out to do just that.

August, 2015

Mesa, Arizona

Dear Madame Marie de Tocqueville,

You have lived in my imagination for the past twenty years. My surname, Le Sueur, will not be a name which will sound strange to you because it was also the surname of Abeé Le Sueur, the tutor of your beloved Alexis. He was from Picardy. I was born in the Channel Island of Jersey, a peculiar to the Crown of England,[134] which means the Islanders are British subjects.

I am writing to you from my home in America, now known as the United States of America. It all sounds totally confusing: searching for you was equally challenging!

---

[134] http://www.merriam-webster.com/dictionary/peculiar

Madame, your desire to disappear from our world was masterful. It took me seven plus years of determined and at what at times seemed impossible research to find you and your remarkable family in Portsmouth!

In a sense, the Mottleys have become my family. In this book I have written about you, I am inviting you to meet all of them through my eyes, my mind and my heart. I feel a sincere affection for all of them. They, like you, have helped me to understand the world you and Alexis lived in and shared.

In the year 2015, the year in which I am compiling this book for publication, your husband, Alexis de Tocqueville, is even more celebrated than either of you could ever have imagined.

And Madame, much of his life story reflects the love and support you offered him. He continues to be admired by historians all over the world. He is quoted so often, his ideas, his words have become a permanent part of every historian's account of the development of 19th century France and America.

It was my interest in the subject of democracy, Alexis's passion, which brought us together after I retired. Yes, women work, vote and make a vital contribution to society!—my instinct tells me that in our time you would have made a significant contribution to society both here and abroad.

During my search for you I visited Royal Hospital Haslar where you were born and walked through the door to your father's former office! Madame, I walked in your footsteps in Alverstoke, Springfield, and I visited Versailles in France, where you lived with your Aunt and Uncle Belam. My visit to Château de Tocqueville in Normandy was especially memorable, thanks to the current Count de Tocqueville and his lovely wife and family.

At times I have almost felt as though I am one of the family. In fact I know the members of the Mottley family so well, if I woke up and found them in my house, I would get up, make a cup of tea and join the conversation.

The Mottleys, the Belams and the Tocquevilles have opened the door to the19th century and given me insights I never would have had. I sincerely hope the readers of this book will experience the excitement and joy I encountered throughout my mission of bringing you into the light and to your rightful place, beside your beloved husband, Alexis de Tocqueville.

I am

Sincerely and Devotedly Yours,

Sheila Le Sueur

Sheila Le Sueur

Sheila Le Sueur

Sheila Le Sueur was born on the Channel Island of Jersey in 1927, located 14 miles from the coast of Normandy, France. When King John lost his French possessions in 1215, the islands of Jersey and Guernsey elected to remain with the Crown. The islanders are neither English nor French. Originally the native language was French but today most islanders speak English.

Sheila's idyllic childhood was rudely interrupted at the age of 13 when the Nazis seized the Channel Islands. On June 28, 1940, Sheila and four young friends were leaving the beach and soon found themselves running for their lives as a German plane peppered them with bullets. Apparently Hitler had deluded himself into thinking he had conquered part of England by invading the two islands. July 1, 1940 began five long years of enemy Nazi Occupation.

Curfews, severe food rations and military officers everywhere delivered an important message to Sheila and her family. The meaning of freedom suddenly gained a new importance. Survival became their only mission as contact with the rest of the world was cut off. Although the Nazis confiscated all radios, during the final months a number of islanders managed to listen to the news on homemade crystal sets. In Sheila's first book, *Two Flags, One Heart,* Sheila relates the harrowing story of her World War II occupation experience.

Jersey was liberated May 9, 1945, one day after VE Day. The liberators were a combination of Jersey troops in the British Armed Forces and the American Naval Armed Forces.

After the Occupation, Sheila left the island to attend nursing school at the Royal London Hospital. She returned to Jersey as a Registered nurse and worked in the General Hospital for almost three years. At the age of 25, Sheila answered an ad for a nursing position in Detroit, Michigan. As soon as she resettled in the United States, she set forth on another adventure that lasted for the rest of her life. Eventually she became a naturalized citizen of the United States.

Alexis de Tocqueville's observations in his book *Democracy in America* fueled Sheila's interest in the democratic process. Her desire to become a more informed voter led to further introspection about the value of freedom. Says Sheila: "There is one absolute in all of our lives. We have no choice of parents, ethnic origin, village, town, or country. In that way, we are truly equal. From that time on, however, our lives are as different as our fingerprints. We are free to live our days as we choose." Sheila's life is a testimony to this observation.

Other Books by Sheila Le Sueur:

Two Flags, One Heart, Starlight Publishing, 2000. [World War II Occupation on the Island of Jersey]

The Bon Secours Hospital Holden Coronary Care Unit, Mesa AZ: Dandelion Books, 2010. [Nursing experiences in the US]

Claudine Martin-Yurth

Normandy, France in 1943 was not a good time to be born into the world, but this was when Claudine Madeleine Marie-Louise made her appearance. At age 16, upon graduating from the Lycée of Louviers (French high school) she was granted an AFS scholarship to spend a year in an American high school as an exchange student. Her adventurous spirit now awakened, instead of following in her family's footsteps and becoming a school teacher, she spent three years in London teaching French.

In 1971 Claudine emigrated to Idaho where she survived as a seamstress, a chef and restaurant owner. In the '80s the call of the wild took her to the back country in Idaho and Alaska as an assistant guide and cook for Sun Valley Trekking, an expedition organization. This led to the writing of an outdoors cookbook, *The Trekking Chef,* published in 1989 by Lyons & Burford (reissued in 1995 by Globe Pequot).

Claudine then moved to Salt Lake City, Utah, where she studied Ayurvedic medicine, taught yoga and married inventor, scientist and author Dave Yurth. She now enjoys non-retirement gardening, cooking, looking after six rescued cats and volunteering at Best Friends Animal Sanctuary's kitten nursery.

Acknowledgments

I wish to acknowledge and thank so many people who helped and encouraged me along the way. They include:

Madame Marie de Tocqueville (Mary Mottley) who just wouldn't let go of my mind;

Bruce Barnes, a very helpful librarian;

John Lukacs, determined and encouraging;

Mesa Community College New Frontiers for Learning in Retirement;

Marjorie Bloy, English historian and a great supporter;

Anthony Adolph, genealogist, writer, broadcaster and researcher, who provided copious documents regarding the Mottley family in Portsmouth, England (wwww.anthonyadolph.co.uk);

Annette Potter, A dear friend and Portsmouth native;

Jean-Louis Benoît, a philosopher and gentle man, who devoted his life work to researching and writing books about Alexis de Tocqueville (in his works about Tocqueville, Dr. Benoît refers to Mary Mottley as Mme. de Tocqueville); thanks to Dr. Benoît, we were able to obtain a copy of *Oeuvres complètes, tome 14 : Correspondance familiale* [*Volume XIV, Family Correspondence,* Gallimard (24 mars 1998)], which is only one volume of Dr. Benoît's comprehensive work about Alexis de Tocqueville. http://www.amazon.fr/Alexis-Tocqueville-compl%C3%A8tes-Correspondance-familiale/dp/2070750655/ref=sr_1_16?ie=UTF8&qid=1439991737&sr=8-16&keywords=jean-louis+benoit. This volume contains many letters from Alexis to his wife, of which are translated excerpts included in Chapter 9 of this book (translated by Claudine Martin-Yurth);

Michael Barone, senior political analyst for the *Washington Examiner* and a resident fellow at the American Enterprise Institute;

Jonathan Evans, Jonathan Evans, Archivist, The Royal London Hospital Museum & Archives;

John Sinel, friend;

Clare Ash and her book connection to Mary Mottley;

Fred Brown, Professor Emeritus, Stony Brook University, NY;

Richard Royer, MD, enthusiastic supporter for many, many years;

Jean Paul Madelent, a connected friend;

C-SPAN for sparking my interest;

Archives St. Lô;

Societe Jersaise;

John von Heyking, political science professor and supporter;

Laurent Quevilly, supportive French journalist;

George and Janet Gaudin, dear friends who always leave a car for me on the dock at St. Malo;

Jean Paul Madelenat, a life-long friend;

Estelle Egglishaw, wonderful friend and travel companion;

Martin Sommerness, NAU professor and *C-SPAN* connection.

Joseph Epstein, a gentle man and respected essayist;

Thomas Pavel, professor, kind and easy to know;

Vicki Chavarria at the UPS store, cheerful, helpful, and professional;

Lisa Rowe, friend and neighbor;

Sonia and Francis Hamon, wonderfully supportive Jersey friends;

Claudine Martin-Yurth, who did such a splendid job translating several of Alexis's letters to Mary, adding a very special touch to this book;

Carol Adler, who convinced me I might be able to write;

Last but not least, I would like to acknowledge the love and support and encouragement of my family: My sister Anne, my nieces Patricia, Michele, Sheila, Alison, and my nephew Matthew.

Photographs and Graphics:

Royal Hospital Haslar – Door to George Mottley's Office – Courtesy of Eric Birbeck and the Haslar Heritage Group

Tocqueville Château Photos & Portrait of Alexis de Tocqueville – Courtesy of Archives départementales de la Manche

Portrait of Mme. Marie de Tocqueville, Mary Mottley – Courtesy of the National Library of France

Scanned copies of Alexis de Tocqueville's letters to his wife, Mary Mottley – Courtesy of Archives départementales de la Manche

Original letters of Alexis de Tocqueville to his wife, Mary Mottley (excerpts) – Courtesy of Edition Gallimard, *Vol. XIV, Family Correspondence*, collected by Jean-Louis Benoît

Bibliography

Benoît, Jean-Louis. *Tocqueville,* Perrin. 2013.

Brogan, Hugh. *Alexis de Tocqueville, A Life*. New Haven, CT: Yale University Press, 2006.

Brown, Frederick. *Alexis de Tocqueville, Letters from America.* Yale University Press, 2010.

Epstein, Joseph. *Alexis de Tocqueville (Eminent Lives)*. New York: Harper, 2006.

Jardin, Andre. *Tocqueville: A Biography*. New York: Farrar, Straus and Giroux, 1989.

Pierson, George Wilson. *Tocqueville in America*. New York: Oxford University Press, 1938.

Tocqueville, Alexis de, *Democracy in America.* Liberty Fund, Inc. New Edition English, 2012.